Keep Hope Alive!
Super Tuesday and Jesse Jackson's 1988 Campaign for the Presidency

Penn Kimball

Joint Center for Political and Economic Studies Press,
Washington, D.C.

The Joint Center for Political and Economic Studies contributes to the national interest by helping black Americans participate fully and effectively in the political and economic life of our society. A nonpartisan, nonprofit institute founded in 1970, the Joint Center uses research and information dissemination to accomplish three objectives: to improve the socioeconomic status of black Americans; to increase their influence in the political and public policy arenas; and to facilitate the building of coalitions across racial lines.

Copyright © 1992 by Penn Kimball
Foreword copyright 1992 by the Joint Center for Political and Economic Studies, Inc.

1301 Pennsylvania Avenue, Suite 400
Washington, D.C. 20004 202-626-3500

Distributed by arrangement with
National Book Network
4720 Boston Way
Lanham, MD 20706

3 Henrietta Street
London WC2E 8LU England

Library of Congress Cataloging-in-Publication Data

Kimball, Penn.
"Keep Hope Alive!" : Super Tuesday and Jesse Jackson's
1988 Campaign for the Presidency / by Penn Kimball.
p.   cm.
Includes index.
1. Presidents—United States—Election—1988.
2. Jackson, Jesse, 1941- . 3. Afro-Americans—Politics
and government.   4. United States—Politics and
government—1981-1989.   I. Title
E880.K56   1991   324.973' 0927—dc20   91-75486 CIP

ISBN 0-941410-68-4 (cloth : alk. paper)

For Julie

Contents

The Emerging
Black Politics

During the quarter century since passage of the Voting
Rights Act, the growth of black political power has been both
a barometer of change and a strategic weapon in the continuing struggle for full equality.

By virtually any measure, blacks have made giant strides
toward full participation in the political process since 1965.
Black Americans and their allies have torn down all of the
official obstacles to voting and have eliminated most of the
devices that diluted black votes. Black candidates have attained elected offices at every level of government except the
presidency and vice presidency. In relative voting terms, the
gap between blacks and whites has narrowed from over 12
percentage points to about four points. The ranks of black
elected officials have swelled from fewer than 500 black
elected officials in 1965 to more than 7,500 today. In the
capital of the Old Confederacy, L. Douglas Wilder serves as
governor. In our nation's two largest cities, New York and
Los Angeles—as in Philadelphia, Detroit, Washington, D.C.,
and more than 300 other cities across the country—black
men and women serve as mayors. In November 1990, voters

Just as a quarter century ago, when the cutting edge of the civil rights movement shifted from protest to politics, we are now witnessing an equally momentous change—from the margins to the mainstream of the American political system.

elected 26 black members to the U.S. House of Representatives, including the first black Republican in more than half a century.

While the presidency and vice presidency have so far eluded blacks, the 1984 and 1988 Jesse Jackson presidential candidacies, the Wilder and Dinkins elections, and the selection of Ron Brown as chairman of the Democratic National Committee all suggest that the nation's highest offices may not be beyond reach. The road to these offices may also be paved with political successes at the state and local levels where black influence is growing significantly.

These achievements are harbingers of a growing trend in black politics, one that marks a shift in both focus and strategies. Whereas for two decades the principal thrust of black politics has been to secure black representation for predominantly black constituencies, today's black political aspirants seek leadership positions in the mainstream of American politics.

With the election in 1990 of William Jefferson to the New Orleans congressional seat previously held by Lindy Boggs, blacks held every congressional seat in the nation where there is a black majority. Similar growth in black representation is coming to a crest at every level of politics, from school boards to city halls to state houses. This trend, which will continue as the black population becomes more concentrated in certain political jurisdictions, is not new. Rather it is the logical outgrowth of population distribution and years of organizing and mobilizing the black vote.

What is new today, however, is the breakthrough blacks

are beginning to make in predominantly white jurisdictions—the phenomenon journalists have dubbed "crossover" politics. This new mainstreaming of black politics has enormous implications for the nation's political process and for the vitality of our society. Like most "new" trends, this one is rooted in the events of the past, the opportunities of the present, and the imperatives of the future.

There are important precedents for the kind of politics we see emerging today. More than a century ago, blacks held statewide offices in the South during Reconstruction. A quarter century ago, a black Republican, Edward Brooke, made history when he was elected to the United States Senate from Massachusetts. Another milestone came in 1973, when Tom Bradley won election as mayor of Los Angeles, a city whose electorate is less than 20 percent black.

Mayor Bradley may have become the contemporary role model for a new breed of black elected officials whose base is in the black community but who can also win the support of whites, Latinos, Asian-Americans, Jews, and other segments of our diverse society. The Bradley model became even more salient when he almost won the governorship of California in 1982.

The dawn of the 1990s brought more examples of this new breed of political leader: Wilder, Dinkins, Mayor Norman Rice of Seattle, Mayor John Daniels of New Haven—the list keeps growing. Even in North Carolina, senatorial candidate Harvey Gantt carried 35 percent of the white vote despite Jesse Helms' racist demagoguery. And within three months after Gantt's defeat, a black legislator, Daniel Blue, was elected speaker of that state's house of representatives.

From the Margins to the Mainstream

Just as a quarter century ago, when the cutting edge of the civil rights movement shifted from protest to politics, we are now witnessing an equally momentous change—from the margins to the mainstream of the American political system.

"Keep Hope Alive!"

Blacks today are no longer limited to the political periphery. After more than a century of struggle, they have gained access to the political system; after decades of painstaking organizing, they have built a formidable base in predominantly black communities; and now, they are building coalitions across racial lines, winning public offices in predominantly white jurisdictions and capturing leadership positions that can influence the full spectrum of public policies—from civil rights and human services to economics, foreign policy, and national security. Perhaps no two events reflect the change in black politics so clearly as the two campaigns by Jesse Jackson, in 1984 and 1988, for the presidency. Jackson's 1984 strategy rested primarily on the two cornerstones of traditional black politics: voter registration and mobilization. Four years later, Jackson ran a very different campaign, one based on an appeal to a "rainbow" coalition with shared economic and social interests.

There are three generalizations that can be drawn about the emerging black politics. First, and perhaps foremost, it is a politics of inclusion, a politics that reaches across the barriers of race, ethnicity, and color. It is a politics that encompasses the protection of basic rights, to be sure, but it also envisions the achievement of other hopes and aspirations in concert with the pursuit of the larger goals of the nation as a whole. In the words of Louis Martin, the Godfather of black politics, it is a politics that "draws the larger circle." This is the kind of inclusiveness that characterized the campaigns of Wilder, Dinkins, Bradley, and Gantt.

Inclusiveness was also one of the hallmarks of the Jackson 1988 presidential campaign. While in 1984 Jackson stressed his concern for the disadvantaged in America, in 1988 he also called for policies that addressed the entire electorate. He campaigned against factory closings and farm foreclosures; he marched in picket lines in urban ethnic neighborhoods and opened campaign headquarters in rural Iowa; his staff included Hispanics, Jews, and Asian-Americans, Northerners and Southerners. He carried Michigan and he made strong showings in Vermont, Hawaii, Maine, and Wisconsin—states with relatively small black populations.

The second generalization we can make about the new black politics is that it differs in tone and temper from the politics of the sixties. While it remains firmly grounded in moral values, it is no longer a politics based primarily on civil rights laws and moral suasion. This is not to say that the issues of access to employment and health care are not as morally compelling as the issues of access to voting rights and public accommodations; but there is room for honest disagreement and principled compromise on the policy issues of the nineties. This was not always the case with the issues of the sixties. Thus, today blacks pursue their priorities not only with appeals to conscience but also with appeals to enlightened self-interest. Moreover, the appeals are not characterized by non-negotiable demands but by the give-and-take of traditional politics.

Third, the emerging black politics is increasingly the politics of a new generation. Of course, many of our political pacesetters, including Jesse Jackson, are indeed veterans of the struggles of the sixties. But, increasingly, black political leaders—those with multiracial constituencies as well as those in heavily black jurisdictions—will be men and women who proudly proclaim their gratitude to the civil rights movement but who were born too late to participate in it. When the Voting Rights Act was passed in 1965, for example, Congressmen Mike Espy of Mississippi and Alan Wheat of Missouri were teenagers. Inevitably, this new generation of leadership will have a different style, a different vocabulary, and even different priorities from the generations that preceded it.

The Challenge of Diversity

The continuing evolution in black politics is shaped not only by generational change but by demographic change, as well. By the beginning of the next century, four out of every five people entering the American work force will be minorities, women, and immigrants. One in every five Americans will be a racial or ethnic minority or a recent immigrant. In fact, in the next century the phrase "racial minority" may become less meaningful because no racial, ethnic, or color group will comprise an absolute majority of Americans. In many political jurisdictions today we already find a majority of minorities.

These changes imply that those who would attract "crossover" votes must be attentive not only to the line which divides black and white, but also to the barriers between blacks and other racial and ethnic groups. While all political leaders should reach out to every group within our society, such outreach is becoming, more and more, a matter of political necessity as well. It is particularly important for black political leaders whose traditional bases in central cities are increasingly being integrated by Latinos and Asians. Despite differences in heritage and culture, all these groups share common concerns such as job opportunities, better schools, affordable housing and health care, and safe streets.

In this changing environment, black politicians are challenged to show the same cultural sensitivity to other minorities that we ask them and white politicians to show to us. New political styles and pragmatic coalitions are needed to achieve mutual goals in the era of multiracial and multicultural politics.

The Future of Black Politics

Whether the mainstream strategies that are emerging today will in fact become the dominant thrust of black political empowerment in the years ahead or will give way to some other approach, including—quite possibly—a reversion to protest politics, will depend in large measure on two factors. One is how mainstream politics plays in the larger black community; and the other is whether it leads to significant improvements in the social and economic status

As Jesse Jackson explains, the majority of black Americans have the same needs as the majority of Americans of every race: good jobs at good wages; health insurance for our families; decent, drug-free schools for our children.

of the black population.

To be sure there is a lively, healthy, and sometimes confrontational debate within the black community today about the consequences—and the costs—of this evolution in black politics. A few influential blacks question whether the prize is worth the price. They see "mainstream politics" as a device for distracting black public officials from black concerns and for co-opting the black electorate in a national political system that often ignores their hopes and aspirations.

From a black perspective, each of these dangers is real; but none need be inevitable.

First, and most importantly, these trends need not amount to what Howard University Professor Ron Walters has provocatively called "the death of black politics." Predominantly black constituencies will continue to exist, and they will continue to elect effective and aggressive leadership in the tradition of Adam Clayton Powell, Shirley Chisholm, and Richard Hatcher. And these officials can always be relied on to articulate the black agenda in its boldest form.

The mainstreaming of black politics, in fact, serves to increase rather than compromise black political power, while allowing for expanded black political participation beyond constituencies with heavy black majorities. Indeed, many of the forerunners of what has been called crossover politics —including Harold Washington, Tom Bradley, Douglas Wilder, and David Dinkins—all had their roots in the politics of overwhelmingly black communities. As these politicians have demonstrated, crossover politics most certainly need not mean abandoning the black community.

As Jesse Jackson explains so effectively, the majority of

black Americans have the same needs as the majority of Americans of every race: good jobs at good wages; health insurance for our families; decent, drug-free schools for our children—these priorities have universal appeal. They are more likely to be achieved by a broad-gauged policy coalition. In short, what we see on the horizon is not the death of black politics but its growth and maturation.

The question for the future is not only whether black political leaders will appeal to the larger society, but also how the larger society will respond. Race remains a potent factor in politics, as the Republicans' "Willie Horton" ads or Senator Jesse Helms' anti-affirmative action ads amply demonstrate. As Professor Kimball points out in this account of Jackson's 1988 bid for the presidency, black aspirants who run for public office must also run an obstacle course defined by race. Jackson's pursuit of a "rainbow coalition" was an attempt to reach across the barriers of race, ethnicity, color, and station to appeal to voters at those critical junctures where various interests intersect. The extent to which he succeeded offers hope to all those who enter this changing political arena. The extent to which he failed defines the challenges that must be met.

As we move into an era of dramatic demographic changes in the labor force, in the electorate, and in our multicolored and multicultural society, we are all being challenged to appreciate the fact that increasingly the politics of democracy is the politics of diversity. And through the new politics of inclusion, blacks are addressing issues that are vital not only to them but to all Americans.

Eddie N. Williams
President
Joint Center for Political
and Economic Studies

July 1991

You must not surrender.
You may or may not get there,
but just know that you're qualified
and hold on and hold out.
We must never surrender . . . .
Keep hope alive! Keep hope alive!
Keep hope alive!

Jesse Jackson

Introduction

The idea of doing a study of Super Tuesday—the regional presidential primary held in 14 Southern and border states on a common date in March 1988—was prompted, first, by the significance of this latest experiment in the changing process by which American political parties nominate their candidates for president of the United States.

Pressure, beginning in the 1960s, to reform a system whereby party insiders controlled a convention of hand-picked delegates produced, by the 1970s, a proliferation of statewide presidential primaries across the country. Within the Democratic Party, reforms were accelerated by opposition to the Vietnam war and by the presidential candidacies of Eugene McCarthy, Robert Kennedy, and George McGovern. Women, minorities, and labor unions saw a more open process as a way to win a fairer share of convention delegates. On the Republican side, the nomination of Barry Goldwater and then Ronald Reagan had been sealed by delegates elected in the grassroots amid a feeling that Eastern elitists, out of touch with conservative sentiments in the hinterlands, held too much power in the convention's selection of presidential candidates.

Despite some major reforms, there was a widespread sense that the presidential primary system had serious short-

1

Super Tuesday was largely the invention of Southern state legislators seeking to restore the region's one-time leading position in forming the Democratic Party's national ticket.

comings. The traditional primary calendar made Iowa and New Hampshire—with no claims to be representative of the rest of the nation—the first states to winnow the field of candidates and thus the focus of major media attention. The presidential campaign period went on so long that candidates sometimes became exhausted, and their expenses became so prohibitive that, despite public financing, presidential hopefuls became hostages to special interests in order to finance the ballooning costs of politics. Moreover, the random geographical spread and timing of these trial heats diluted the influence of regional politics and issues.

This feeling of regional deprivation was particularly strong in the South. Super Tuesday was largely the invention of Southern state legislators seeking to restore the region's one-time leading position within the Democratic Party in the formulation of presidential platforms and the composition of the national ticket. It also held appeal for those who wanted to experiment with a more orderly and representative method for selecting presidential candidates.

In reality, Super Tuesday fulfilled few of the expectations of its sponsors. The prospects for this and similar regional presidential primaries in the future do not appear to have been enhanced by the experience in 1988. Yet it became the springboard for a remarkable new development in American presidential politics.

The wild card practically ignored by the architects of Super Tuesday was the Rev. Jesse L. Jackson, born in South Carolina, educated in North Carolina, and a marcher across the South in the civil rights movement led by the late Rev. Martin Luther King, Jr. Although he had campaigned for the presidency four years before and had won more than 400 delegates to the Democratic convention in San Francisco, Jesse Jackson was not taken very seriously at the beginning of 1988 by either the politicians or the press.

There were good reasons to be skeptical about a Jackson candidacy. First and foremost was the question whether any African-American seeking national office could muster sufficient white support to have a chance of winning. Jackson's dream of mobilizing a liberal, interracial Rainbow Coalition depended on registering and turning out large numbers of minority voters without frightening or antagonizing too large a slice of the white majority, a dilemma which has faced virtually all African-Americans seeking election outside their home base.

Also in doubt, and central to Jackson's Rainbow Coalition strategy, was whether enough pieces of the New Deal coalition could be united and become once again a potent progressive force.

In a bland field of cautious politicians, Jackson came across as a forthright, compassionate advocate on a range of important issues. Almost alone among Democratic presidential candidates, Jackson took bold stands in favor of new programs for housing, welfare, and education; he urged taxing the rich to help the poor; he gave top priority to the fight against drugs; he favored smaller defense budgets and stronger initiatives for peace in Central America and the Middle East; he unequivocally supported the right of women to choose whether or not to have an abortion. But these were not positions that appealed to every taste. Jackson stirred the emotions, negative as well as positive.

Then there was also the question of Jackson's "hot" personality, his lack of practical experience in elected office, his one-time association with the demagogue Louis Farrakhan, and his own remarks about "Hymietown" when referring to New York City in a background session with reporters in 1984. To many political observers, there was little expectation that a candidate carrying all this baggage would emerge as a serious factor in the presidential sweepstakes.

But Jackson's campaign in the primary states of the Old Confederacy benefited from some happy coincidences. His principal competition was split between two white candidates, Massachusetts Governor Michael Dukakis and Tennessee Senator Albert Gore, Jr., neither of whom had the national reputation or credentials of such 1984 opponents as Walter Mondale, George McGovern, or Gary Hart. Also unlike 1984, he did not have to compete for the support of the region's substantial bloc of African-American voters. Finally, a spirited Republican primary to pick a successor to Ronald Reagan promised to attract conservative whites who might otherwise be voting against Jackson in the Democratic contest.

Yet few were prepared for the responsiveness of audiences to Jesse Jackson's charismatic campaign. His well-honed message struck a chord not only among African-Americans bursting with racial pride but among young people, generally, on college campuses, and among champions of certain deeply felt causes such as opposition to nuclear weapons or nuclear power. His showing in Northern states just before and just after he captured nearly a third of the delegates elected on Super Tuesday converted his role as a rank outsider to that of a serious player in Democratic presidential politics. For a brief moment serious speculation centered on the possibility that an African-American in the year 1988 might actually win the presidential nomination of a major political party.

The road after Super Tuesday, however, exposed pitfalls which were foreshadowed by a close examination of what really took place during the great Super Tuesday experiment. Jackson polled less than 10 percent of the white vote on Super Tuesday and did best with white voters elsewhere in relatively small states unthreatened by large populations of African-Americans competing for jobs, places in the schools, or housing in segregated neighborhoods. These results remind one of the long-standing debate over whether

4

it is class, race, or personality that prevents some white Americans from voting for African-American candidates. In addition to lack of white support, African-American registration and turnout for even the charismatic Jesse Jackson was not exceptionally high in 1988 and actually decreased from 1984 in some places. My own research on minority registration (*The Disconnected*, Columbia University Press, 1972) has indicated that even when registration barriers are removed there is an invisible ceiling of participation for minority voters which has proved difficult to pierce. How relevant to their needs do the disadvantaged find the cacophony of elections? And since younger voters participate least in voting, the fact that minority groups have a lower average age than whites may be another inhibiting factor.

Although more and more African-American, Latino, and other minority candidates have been winning local elections with the help of white support, it doesn't always happen. The success in 1989 of L. Douglas Wilder in being elected governor of the Commonwealth of Virginia, albeit by the narrowest of margins, was followed by the decisive defeat of Andrew Young in 1990 by a white candidate for the Democratic nomination for governor of Georgia. Both Wilder and Young abstained from supporting Jesse Jackson in 1988, yet both felt encouraged by his showing to test their own chances.

As a role model for a new cohort of African-Americans seeking important elective office, Jackson irritated some voters, white and black, with his exuberant style, and he offended other constituencies by his uncompromising positions. But the legacy of his 1988 campaign for the presidency continues to be felt, keeping alive the hopes for African-Americans to achieve high office in America.

This book is based on firsthand observations along the 1988 Jackson campaign trail from Alabama to New York. My wife, Julie Ellis, who is also a journalist, and I drove through the South from January through Super Tuesday and returned for the Democratic convention in Atlanta in July. Along the way, we talked to academics, political reporters, politicians, and campaign workers for the candidates. As a former journalism professor, I was fortunate to have access to the experiences of former students who were covering Jackson, Dukakis, Gore, Bush, and other candidates in various parts of the country. I deliberately refrained from trying to interview Jackson during the primaries, preferring to concentrate on the perspective of voters and trying to be a more or less inconspicuous observer.

I have been an urban reporter, editor, and teacher for half a century and wrote a book 20 years ago about minority participation in American politics. For this study, I enjoyed the sponsorship of the Joint Center for Political and Economic Studies in Washington, D.C., which opened doors for me among many African-American elected officials. As I used to tell my students, it is impossible to be unbiased but the goal of a good reporter is to be fair. I have tried my best.

Breakthrough at the Polls?

Jesse Jackson's 1988 quest for the presidency was the culmination of two decades of striving by African-Americans to win places of power within the ranks of elected officials. The first significant breakthrough for blacks was registered in 1966 when Republican Edward Brooke in Massachusetts became the first (and so far, only) member of his race to be elected to the United States Senate since Reconstruction. In 1967, Democrats Richard Hatcher and Carl Stokes were elected mayor in two Northern cities, Gary, Indiana, and Cleveland, Ohio. The success of Brooke in winning a constituency in which African-Americans were only a tiny minority and of Stokes in obtaining a significant proportion of white voters in a multi-ethnic, urban metropolis posed the prospect of widespread gains for African-Americans seeking elected office.

The styles and personalities of Brooke and Stokes were similar: cool and reassuring, soft-spoken, and moderate. Both came up through the ranks of party service within regular organizations, first contesting and winning lower

> Jackson's charismatic personality, his evangelical speaking style, and his commitment to those excluded from the mainstream of society lifted him above the level of conventional politicians.

offices. Neither publicly engaged in the hot rhetoric of racial awareness and social change. Both cultivated the support of business organizations, newspaper publishers, and other segments of the white establishment. Their triumphs were hailed as symbols that an era of racial harmony might be at hand.

The model was replicated in subsequent years by the successful candidacies for mayor of Kenneth Gibson in Newark (New Jersey), Tom Bradley in Los Angeles, and Maynard Jackson in Atlanta. All won with significant support from white voters.

Jesse Jackson, who first declared for the presidency in 1984, was a minority candidate of a different stripe, and his approach to politics involved a strategy different from the more laid-back style of these predecessors.

One of the key assumptions of Jackson's Rainbow Coalition was that there remained a vast pool of unregistered Americans who, if they could be added to the voting lists and energized behind a candidate unafraid to espouse their interests, could tip the balance of power away from the cautious middle-of-the-roaders who seemed to fare best among the traditionally enfranchised. Another assumption was that a substantial segment of white America was ready and willing to vote for an African-American who spelled out the common ground shared by both races.

Jackson's charismatic personality, his evangelical speaking style, and his commitment to those excluded from the mainstream of society lifted him above the level of conventional politicians. The price might be to frighten some white voters who had been assuaged by the low-key campaigns of a Stokes, Brooke, or Bradley, but the reward might be an outpouring of voters, white and black, responding to a candidate who came down hard on the issues which most strongly appealed to feminists, union members, embattled farmers, peace advocates, and those cut out from the economic and social opportunities accorded to other Americans.

The election of African-Americans to public office in the United States received significant impetus from the Voting Rights Act of 1965. That piece of legislation was the culmination of a decade of civil rights activity triggered after the 1954 decision by the Supreme Court outlawing segregation in the public schools. Protests in the South in the fifties and sixties focused national attention on discrimination against African-Americans not only in the public schools, but also in restaurants, transportation, housing, and the work place.

Television news accounts of white police violence against peaceful demonstrations by blacks—such as one demonstration in Birmingham, Alabama, and another led by the Rev. Martin Luther King, Jr., at Selma, Alabama—aroused the conscience of citizens all over the country. With the passage of federal legislation promising equal access to the polls, expectations rose for an increasing presence of African-Americans in the political system.

At the same time, frustration over the lack of economic opportunity for African-Americans living in dense, segregated urban areas boiled over into a series of urban riots during the long hot summers of 1965 to 1967 in Los Angeles, Detroit, Cleveland, and Newark. After these upheavals and the assassination of Dr. King, the philosophy of peaceful protest gave way to militant expressions of black power. The 1968 report of the Kerner Commission deplored the existence of two Americas, one white and one black, splitting the fragile fabric of the Republic. It portrayed the issue of civil rights not only as a moral question but as crucial to the survival of our political and economic system. The self-interest as well as the moral principles of the country's white majority were in danger of being undermined.

In a climate in which white liberal idealism for racial integration was mixed with fear over the consequences of continued segregation, black candidates in the seventies won coalition victories in local elections as far apart as Cleveland, Atlanta, and Los Angeles. African-Americans in Southern districts where newly enfranchised blacks constituted a critical mass of the electorate won election to county offices, city councils, state legislatures, and Congress. African-Americans won statewide positions as high as lieutenant governor and attorney general, but Mayor Tom Bradley of Los Angeles was twice rejected in attempts to win the governorship of California. Token votes for presidential nominee were cast in Democratic national conventions for New York Congresswoman Shirley Chisholm and Georgia State Representative Julian Bond. But until Jesse Jackson announced his candidacy for the Democratic nomination for president in 1984, the breakthrough in thinking had not yet occurred when an African-American might be considered a serious contender for the top office in the land.

Even Jackson, according to African-American politicians, regarded his 1984 candidacy as largely symbolic, seizing the opportunity to register new black voters and raise their consciousness. He wanted them to understand that they could hold the balance of power in future election contests between white candidates for state and national office.

Next time around, Jackson's announcement for the Democratic nomination once again would put to the test the ability of an African-American candidate to be considered a serious possibility for election to the White House. This time, after four years of continuous organizational activity, Jackson announced on October 24, 1987, "I want to be elected president of the United States of America."

It was indeed an ambitious goal. In the first place, the number of states scheduled to hold presidential primaries had risen in 1988 to 35, a formidable number of contests for any serious candidate. When Senator John F. Kennedy managed to win the nomination as an outsider in 1960, he had to prove his vote-getting prowess in only a handful of states. Was it reasonable to expect that an African-American with no public office of his own could mount an all-out, nationwide contest? Jackson had come to the 1984 Democratic convention with 466 delegates of 3,933. He would need a great many more to become a serious player at Atlanta in 1988, where 2,081 delegates would constitute a majority.

The introduction of an experimental, regional primary in Southern states, all to be held on the first Tuesday in March, added a new factor to the equation. If there was a core African-American vote anywhere it was in the 14 Super Tuesday states south of the Mason-Dixon Line. The voting there would come early in the campaign season. How would Jackson fare in this innovation? Many white Democrats in the South had crossed party lines to vote twice for Republican Ronald Reagan. Would Jackson's candidacy affect Democratic chances in November? Even if Jackson succeeded among fellow African-Americans, could he hold an appreciable number of white primary voters?

Furthermore, minority politics in the United States had expanded far beyond activating a core of African-American voters. Politically conscious ethnic groups now included a fast-growing segment of Latinos in delegate-rich states—Mexican-Americans in Texas and California, Caribbean Hispanics in Florida, Puerto Ricans in New York. How realistic was the goal of a Rainbow Coalition when black and brown often competed with one another for a place at the table?

With 1,121 delegates at stake on Super Tuesday, a good showing by Jackson might translate into acceptance of him by the national media as a serious candidate. In a race with no incumbent president and several white hopefuls, Jackson needed only a modest white vote in addition to a supposedly solid black base to become a contender in the delegate sweepstakes. In primaries outside the South, where racial considerations had not been a historical part of politics, the idea of a Rainbow Coalition could then be put to the test in

11

supposedly more favorable circumstances.

Jackson would need to avoid the mistake made by Gary Hart in 1984, who had no game plan for capitalizing on his upset victory in New Hampshire. Hart did not even have qualified delegate slates in many key states, such as Georgia, Pennsylvania, and Illinois, where the filing dates had already passed. Jackson would need to plan ahead to be in a position to build on any early success. By happy coincidence, the first two contests after the returns from Super Tuesday were the Democratic caucus in South Carolina (53 delegates), where Jackson was born, and the primary in Illinois (200) where Jackson now made his home. After that would come a rapid-fire series of crucial tests—in Michigan (162), Wisconsin (91), and New York (292). The primary season would come to a climax in June, when New Jersey (126) and California (363), with a total population of two million African-Americans and 5.9 million Latinos, would vote the same day on opposite coasts. All of this was a grueling prospect for a candidate outside the mainstream with limited financial backing and limited expectations of success by almost everyone except himself. But first, thanks to the challenge provided by the nation's initial regional presidential primary, Jesse Jackson needed to seize the opportunity to make his candidacy credible to the nation.

2

The Law of Unintended Consequences

The event that opened the window of opportunity for Jesse Jackson's 1988 campaign for the Democratic presidential nomination was Super Tuesday—a strategy originally conceived by "moderate" white Southern politicians as a vehicle for enhancing their influence within the Democratic Party. It was hoped that a simultaneous, regional primary on the second Tuesday in March in a group of Southern and border states would produce an influential bloc of delegates in the national nominating convention. It would also provide a vehicle for promoting the candidacy of more acceptable individuals than such "liberal" standard-bearers as George McGovern and Walter Mondale, whose defeats had also hurt local Democratic tickets throughout the South. The original proponents of Super Tuesday thought that an opportunity to win a substantial share of delegates from the South at an early stage of the nominating process might be an attractive inducement to Southern Democrats of the stripe of Virginia's Governor Charles Robb or Georgia's Senator Sam Nunn. All candidates, moreover, would be persuaded to hone messages that would be persuasive to middle-class whites who had voted in large numbers for Ronald Reagan in 1980 and

1984. Furthermore, Super Tuesday would attract a major share of candidates' time, effort, and money to a region thought by Southerners to have been neglected in the past.

An unspoken consideration among many of the architects of Super Tuesday was the fear that the Democratic Party in the South would come to be perceived as the party of blacks while whites would continue to gravitate toward the Republicans. According to data compiled by the Michigan Survey Research Center, in the 11 states of the Old Confederacy, whites who said they had voted for the Republican candidate rose from fewer than 45 percent in 1968 to more than 80 percent in 1972. Ronald Reagan won a majority of their votes, running against former Georgia governor Jimmy Carter in 1980, and received approximately 70 percent against Walter Mondale. In the 1984 presidential primaries, white political leaders had helped to persuade African-American elected officials such as Birmingham's Richard Arrington and Atlanta's Andrew Young to endorse Walter Mondale rather than Jesse Jackson, significantly cutting down Jackson's percentage among African-American voters in these two states. Mondale carried both states, with Jackson running five percentage points behind his totals in North Carolina and Tennessee. Jackson carried only Louisiana, where local politics contributed to a very low white turnout in the Democratic presidential primary. When the idea for Super Tuesday was being hatched, Democratic leaders in Southern state legislatures seemed of the opinion that Jackson's showing in 1984, such as it was, had been exaggerated by low turnouts among white voters. They did not appear to regard Jackson as a serious contender for 1988.

Instead, they talked of creating a playing field where a white candidate with strong appeal in the region would stimulate greater participation by white voters in the Democratic presidential nominating procedure. In the 1986 elections to the U.S. Senate, successful Democrats in the South such as Georgia's Wyche Fowler and North Carolina's Terry Sanford had carried 30 to 40 percent of the white vote together with black support in the 80 to 90 percent range, a combination good enough to win. Democratic senatorial victories in these states and in Florida, Alabama, and Louisiana in 1986 had enabled Democrats to win back control of the U.S. Senate. In a Southern regional primary, it was argued, welfare-state appeals would be subordinated to patriotism, national defense, or law-and-order, issues deemed more suited to local tastes.

When the idea for Super Tuesday was being hatched, Democratic leaders in Southern state legislatures talked of creating a playing field where a white candidate with strong appeal in the region would stimulate greater participation by white voters.

A front-loaded primary date, moreover, appealed to Democratic leaders in states like Texas which traditionally had not voted until the nomination process was nearly over. Financial or electoral support late in the game produced less gratitude, hence access, to candidates whose trial by fire had occurred early in Iowa and New Hampshire or in other Northern primary contests earlier on the schedule. Proponents of Super Tuesday argued that John Glenn, for example, might have fared better in 1984 in the South if his media image had not been so badly tarnished before the voting began in a few scattered states below the Mason-Dixon Line.

Since Democrats controlled all the Southern state legislatures, where the power to change primary rules resided, it was not too difficult to execute the Super Tuesday experiment. (In states with open primaries, Republicans saw an opportunity to recruit crossover Democrats into voting in the GOP contests, softening them up for November.) Southern African-American politicians perceived a chance to boost registration rolls in their own districts as part of the campaign for primary votes, as well as to swell their influence in statewide and national elections. Veterans of Jackson's 1984 Rainbow Coalition kept a low profile, partly because Jesse's own intentions were far from clear during the interim years when Super Tuesday was being considered. All told, 14 Southern and border states—from Maryland to Texas—voted to approve the regional primary on a common date.

The purity of the original idea was diluted by the presence of such atypical states as Florida and Texas alongside more traditional members of the Old South like Georgia and Mississippi. It was difficult to lump border states such as Oklahoma, Missouri, or Kentucky together with Maryland (and its District of Columbia suburbs) into a coherent regional bloc which also included North Carolina and other New South states. The large expanse of territory, it turned out, made it impractical for candidates to linger very long in any single state or to wander very far beyond the airport to make personal contact with the traditionally Democratic white voters whom party leaders hoped to bring back into the fold.

To complicate matters somewhat, South Carolina Democrats refused to abandon party caucuses for a popular primary and chose the Saturday following the communal date agreed upon by the other states for making their presidential preferences known. Republicans in South Carolina agreed to a primary, but chose the Saturday before Super Tuesday for voting. To muddy the waters further, Massachusetts and Rhode Island also chose March 8 for their own state primaries and four Western states—Washington, Idaho, Nevada, and Wyoming—scheduled party caucuses on that date as well.

When the voting returns came in for Super Tuesday, rarely had there been such a spectacular example of the Law of Unintended Consequences. The ultra-liberal (by Southern white standards) governor of the hated Teddy Kennedy's home state of Massachusetts, Michael Dukakis, won 23.5 percent of the vote and 259 delegates, running first in Florida, Texas, and Maryland. A black radical (by Southern white standards), Jesse Jackson, amassed the largest total of delegates (330) and finished first in six states of the Old Confederacy: Louisiana, Mississippi, Alabama, Georgia, South Carolina, and Virginia. The mantle of the conservative white South fell somewhat awkwardly on the shoulders of a border-state Democrat, Albert Gore, Jr., who had a relatively liberal voting record in the U.S. Senate and only turned 40 during the campaign. Although Gore's percentage of the total vote was slightly higher than Jackson's (27.6 percent to 27.3 percent; 318 delegates), his victories were scored for the most part in states adjacent to his home base of Tennessee (Kentucky, North Carolina, Arkansas, and Oklahoma). This hardly added up to the Southern clout envisaged by the architects of Super Tuesday.

Gore concentrated his principal efforts in the Southern primary states, spending as many days there (over 170) as the combined total for the other candidates. In the process, he never managed to make a respectable showing in a single state north of the Mason-Dixon Line. George Bush, who made a clean sweep of the Republican primaries on Super Tuesday, actually spent less time in those states than either of his principal opponents, Senator Robert Dole and the Reverend Pat Robertson. Even so, Southern voters chose to participate in the Republican primaries in unprecedented numbers, over five million. About 13.5 million out of a potential 40 million voters (33.5 percent) participated in the experiment, although there were wide variations between individual states. The very substantial proportion (40 percent) who asked for Republican ballots foreshadowed the G.O.P. turnout in November when the Republican candidate for president carried every Southern state that had participated in Super Tuesday.

Jesse Jackson's showing in the South legitimized him as a serious contestant in the Democratic presidential sweepstakes at the same time that Michael Dukakis established himself as more than a New England favorite son. Neither result had been anticipated when the Southern Legislative

"Keep Hope Alive!"

Conference, long before any candidates had been identified, took up the idea for a regional primary in the South. How the experiment will be altered in 1992 is still open to question, but it is likely that the primary scenario next time will be tailored to fit a set of candidates perceived by white Democratic legislators in the South as more congenial.

3

Setting the Stage

Traveling through the South in the early weeks of 1988, this observer sensed a widespread indifference toward the mega-primary scheduled for the second Tuesday in March. The phrase Super Tuesday itself baffled rank-and-file voters when they were asked about it. With rare exceptions (*The Washington Post* and the *Atlanta Constitution* being two) the national media in January focused their attention almost exclusively on the upcoming Iowa caucuses. Although only a handful of voters would be involved, Iowa furnished the first concrete test of candidate strength among an unusually large field in both parties. In the South, local journalists agreed that it was too early to be writing stories about Super Tuesday, a political event as yet outside the attention span for an overwhelming share of their audience.

Some of the potential excitement was dulled by the fact that the local political establishment on both the Democratic and Republican sides seemed to share the view that the most likely result in November 1988 would be a Republican sweep of the states south of the Mason-Dixon Line.

Republicans expressed the opinion that George Bush would probably lock up the nomination early because he had generous funds and a superior organization, and because of the popularity of his boss, Ronald Reagan. By early 1988, 22 of 27 Southern GOP members of Congress, as well as half the region's members on the Republican National Committee, had endorsed the vice president. Pat Robertson was seen as providing minor nuisance problems, while Bob Dole was perhaps capable of forcing a showdown in North Carolina, where his wife Elizabeth was a native, and in states closest to his own home base in Kansas. At Robertson headquarters in Chesapeake, Virginia, however, there was considerable optimism and a feeling that their candidate was doing a great deal better than supposed. State GOP organizations, well financed and equipped with computer programs for targeting supporters, were not concealing their predisposition in favor of the vice president.

On the Democratic side, the field of Democratic hopefuls—with the exception of Jesse Jackson and Albert Gore, Jr.—were making only hit-and-run forays into the region as they concentrated their personal schedules in Iowa and New Hampshire. While Jackson, too, was making a special investment of time in Iowa farm areas, his supporters perceived this effort as part of a grand strategy to try to broaden his base among white family farmers in the rural South as well. He had formally announced his presidential candidacy in October 1987, before a convention of the Rainbow Coalition in Raleigh, North Carolina. His state coordinators for the South were picked early and were holding planning sessions in January.

In Virginia, an unexpected opening of a U.S. Senate seat had attracted the candidacy of former governor Charles Robb, who was among those originally seen as a possibility for the national ticket by members of the Southern Legislative Conference, one of the early sponsors of Super Tuesday. After some soul-searching, Georgia Senator Sam Nunn also concluded that 1988 was not the year for him to engage in the presidential race. Senator Gore of Tennessee and Representative Richard Gephardt of Missouri were left to seek to lay claim, in accordance with Super Tuesday doctrine, to white voters in the South who had defected to

Ronald Reagan in 1980 and 1984. Gephardt had been endorsed by a large contingent of his colleagues from the South
in the House of Representatives. He was perceived as a
moderate insider with a voting record in favor of Reagan
defense and tax measures, a supporter of tariff protection for
textiles (an industry important to many Southern regions),
and a champion of more benefits for agriculture—the ingre-
dients of a candidate who might be expected to appeal to the
white Southern constituency.

A development which was to have important repercus-
sions was Gephardt's decision in December 1987 to close all
his field outposts in the South and to move his entire staff to
Iowa for a do-or-die effort. His decision to abandon his
Southern effort before it began may have been dictated by
the availability of funds and the need for an early psychological victory in a state next door to his home base. But it
angered Southern supporters and alarmed politicians still on
the fence who felt they needed a presidential candidate,
whether or not he could beat George Bush, who would make
a strong enough race not to drag down Democratic candidates for state office. Gephardt not only pulled out of the
South, but altered his message to that of a populist outsider
supporting liberal positions he had opposed in the past. The
strategy worked in Iowa, but Gephardt's campaign never
got off the ground again in the South.

Senator Gore moved into the vacuum created by Gephardt,
picking up endorsements from Virginia to Texas. Somewhat
callow by Southern political standards, a border-state native
who had been brought up in Washington, D.C., and educated at Harvard, the son of a liberal senator who had been
defeated at the polls, Gore was scarcely a prototype Southern
leader. He began distancing himself, however, from Democratic progressives who had criticized the Reagan defense
budget and the administration's policies in Central America.
He bypassed the Iowa caucuses and limited his public appearances in New Hampshire (although buying substantial
television advertising in hopes of an unexpected showing

21

there), while negotiating support from Southern elected officials anxious not to miss the boat. In television debates with the other Democratic hopefuls, Gore's strategists hoped that his soft accent and cautious positions on issues would make him the most attractive to moderate Southern voters.

From Southern perspectives most of the other remaining white candidates—former Arizona governor Bruce Babbitt, U.S. Senator Paul Simon of Illinois, Governor Michael Dukakis of Massachusetts, and former Colorado senator Gary Hart—seemed unlikely alternatives early in 1988. Hart, who had done well in the South in 1984, had become the butt of late-night comedians for disclosures about his relationship with a former Miami model. Such gossip did not go down well in the Bible Belt. Babbitt, virtually unknown, fared badly in early television debates. Simon, also a stranger in the South, struck many as a throwback to a past era of liberal doctrine. None of these made more than perfunctory personal visits to the South while concentrating their efforts on party voters in Iowa.

Michael Dukakis, a long shot when he entered the race, proved to be the biggest fund-raiser of them all, chiefly from fellow Greek-Americans, Massachusetts interests, and other sources outside the South. His first priority was to achieve some credibility by a decent showing in Iowa and to follow that up with a smashing showing in New Hampshire, next door to his home base and saturated by television and newspapers from Boston. Looking ahead, he sent his stepson John to open a regional headquarters in Atlanta, so that he would be poised (unlike Hart in 1984) to take advantage of the impetus from a New Hampshire victory. The Dukakis camp envisioned an I-95 strategy in which they would take a leaf from their experience in the high-tech suburbs of Boston and focus on young professionals, as well as many immigrants from the North, living in the metropolitan areas along the freeways from the District of Columbia to Miami, such as the Raleigh-Durham-Chapel Hill research triangle in North Carolina and the suburbs of

Atlanta and Jacksonville. An ex-Peace Corps volunteer in Latin America and fluent in Spanish, Dukakis planned special selective efforts among Latino voters in Florida and Texas.

For Jackson the playing field for Super Tuesday offered some unusual advantages. Alone among the chief contenders, he had campaigned over most of the Southern territory during the 1984 primaries. He had followed this up with activities to register new African-American voters and to mobilize them in key Southern contests for the U.S. Senate in the 1986 off-year elections.

Jackson, in truth, had never ceased campaigning in the South from 1984 to 1988. Key members of his Rainbow Coalition were kept on the payroll with the help of local black leaders. A network of African-American churches and clergymen familiar to Jackson since the civil rights struggles of the sixties were available as a nucleus for mobilizing voters behind the first of their race to mount a nationwide campaign for the presidency. The only black among a roster of white Democratic hopefuls fragmenting the rest of the electorate, Jackson's base vote in the South, though only a minority of the total, was large enough and concentrated enough in certain congressional districts that it translated into a substantial bloc of delegates.

Why these political realities did not jar the architects of Super Tuesday is one of those intriguing questions which recur in politics. One reason, perhaps, is that votes cast by minorities in the South, though always significant, tend to be concentrated in areas not important to most locally elected white politicians. In a large statewide turnout of white voters in the South, minority voters may tip the balance, but do not always loom as large in the media coverage of campaigns where "good ol' boys" predominate. The idea that an African-American candidate could make a serious run for the presidency had not received much media credence even after Jackson's candidacy in 1984, which was regarded as a symbolic gesture by many of those who were involved. New

23

York Congressman Charles B. Rangel, who had endorsed Mondale in 1984, was quoted by *The New York Times* on March 23, 1987, as being skeptical of Jackson's chances in 1988: "Jesse says he can be president, but I'm not sure I'm mature enough to accept that." On that same day, Phil Gailey reported in the *Times* that "few Democrats, including many black elected officials, believe that Mr. Jackson has a serious chance of becoming the party's presidential nominee." Covering a meeting of the Southern Legislative Conference, Paul Taylor and Thomas B. Edsall of *The Washington Post* wrote on August 31, 1987, that Jackson "is generally thought to be running a crusade, not a campaign." Almost without exception, the media discounted the Jackson candidacy and Jackson himself as a major factor in the presidential sweepstakes.

> In Atlanta, Mayor Andrew Young and other veterans of the civil rights movement had made no secret of their personal reservations about Jackson.

This time around, however, the Jackson campaign faced fewer problems among African-American leaders in the South. In 1984, several of the most prominent had endorsed Walter Mondale on the strength of his proven civil rights record and on the practical ground that blacks should be careful to preserve their access to the power structure around a likely white nominee. At a convention of black elected officials in Hartford, Connecticut, in December 1987, speakers suggested that this time it was acceptable if their members decided in some cases to cut a deal with the local white power structure, but in no case was such a deal to include any public endorsements of Jackson's rivals.

That is not to say, however, that all was sweetness and light. In Atlanta, Mayor Andrew Young and other veterans of the civil rights movement had made no secret of their personal reservations about Jackson, and some African-American state legislators were closely allied with Georgia's white governor. Since Atlanta was the host city for the 1988 Democratic National Convention, the mayor and some others argued for neutrality so as to maintain an air of impartiality. Also, the Jewish community in Atlanta, which had been an important part of the coalition that first helped blacks to achieve office in Georgia's capital city, remained alienated by Jackson's "Hymietown" reference to New York City during the 1984 campaign. Staff members of the Georgia delegation in Congress expressed concern over the local implications of another Jackson presidential candidacy.

Recognition of the problem was reflected in Jackson's choice of a Jewish national campaign manager, Ohio's Gerald Austin, along with such key advisers as Ann Lewis and Barry Commoner. But ethnic misgivings continued to haunt the Jackson campaign when it moved North after Super Tuesday.

In Alabama, a split remained between those African-American politicians, many of them members of the state legislature, who had backed Jackson in 1984 and those who had endorsed Mondale, many of them older veterans of the struggle for equal opportunity. In states such as Florida and Texas, the strains between Latinos and African-Americans, sometimes rooted in the economic struggle over limited resources, frequently strained the internal relations within the Rainbow Coalition.

Maintaining good communications and a strong liaison between the national headquarters and field operations in a political campaign is never easy. Jackson's personal style compounded some of these difficulties. He altered his personal schedules on the spur of the moment. His penchant for conducting business over the telephone often left associates in the dark. Loyal, long-time supporters had ideas of their own quite independent of the best-laid plans of campaign central. For all that, one could not help but be impressed with the energy and dedication of Jackson forces in the field as

25

they prepared for the crucial test on Super Tuesday.

In an interview over the telephone in Norfolk, Virginia, during a snowstorm in January, Bishop Levi E. Willis, a key Jackson supporter in 1984, warned against starting too early this time. Bishop Willis, leader of a 60-congregation jurisdiction of the Church of God in Christ, as well as a radio talk show host and successful businessman, had organized a surprise victorious sweep of Tidewater Democratic caucuses by Jackson delegates four years before. That unexpected turn of events was one of the factors, according to reporters in Richmond, that persuaded the Virginia legislature to adopt a presidential primary for the first time. (Pat Robertson engineered a similar upset in 1987 at a state conference of the Republican Party.)

The bishop is a powerful figure in Norfolk area politics, and it is almost impossible for outsiders to make an appointment with him or to break through a phalanx of office assistants to reach him on the telephone. This communication gap between the press and campaign policymakers was a characteristic of the Jackson campaign early on. It proved extremely difficult for this writer, calling under the auspices of the Joint Center for Political and Economic Studies, to make contact with Jackson's Washington office during the winter. The same was true at Jackson headquarters in Chicago. This was at a time when one could make a free call from anywhere in the country to 1-800-MIKE and immediately contact someone in the Boston headquarters of the Dukakis campaign. Access was also easy at Gore's elaborate Crystal City headquarters across the Potomac from the Capitol, and a facsimile machine transmitted daily press releases directly to newsrooms across the South.

The bishop, who is on the air himself every morning at six a.m. over the six stations he owns in Virginia and North Carolina and who televises his Sunday services from his Garden of Prayer Temple in Portsmouth, Virginia, might have struck some as overextended. But he cited long experience in mobilizing African-American voters when he warned that it would be a mistake to step up the Super Tuesday crescendo in Virginia too early. He pointed out that the Rainbow Coalition in the Hampton Roads region had played a key role in 1986 in electing white Congressman Owen B. Pickett through a biracial alliance. He said that he felt Jackson was "much stronger in the state than last time" and that the campaign base had been broadened by placing a white attorney in charge of the Washington suburbs in Northern Virginia. "We're playing in their game," he said, "created by those with a desire to nominate someone else." As for African-American voters, he thought it important to whip up enthusiasm as close as possible to election time.

At that juncture, Dukakis had not even opened a Virginia office beyond the banks of the Potomac, although he came to Richmond during December and held a press conference there.

A Gore supporter, Professor John McGlennon of the College of William and Mary in Williamsburg, a one-time congressional candidate himself, said his decision to volunteer for Gore was triggered by the collapse of the Gephardt effort after a disorganized foray in October 1987. He was disappointed, however, by Gore's decision to bypass Iowa and New Hampshire. He said he thought Gore should establish credibility elsewhere before concentrating on the South.

McGlennon thought Gore's chances in Virginia hinged on the ability of his campaign to activate a substantial number of white voters to choose Democratic ballots on primary day. Virginians, he said, might be responsive to his advocacy of programs favorable to the state's considerable defense installations and his stance as a fiscally responsible Washington insider. Whether he might be conservative enough or Southern enough for crusty independents in the Old Dominion, who had more and more been disposed to vote Republican in presidential elections, only time would tell.

Days before Jackson's North Carolina headquarters were slated to open in Raleigh on January 12, North Carolina Senator Terry Sanford and ex-governor Jim Hunt, among others, appeared with Gore for a public endorsement. The Jackson group in North Carolina was incensed, especially at Sanford who had been elected in 1986 with a heavy African-American vote. (Overlooked perhaps was that some Jackson supporters, as well as Jackson himself, had backed Sanford's African-American opponent in the Democratic primary.)

> Jackson sought out white audiences in the South to emphasize the multiracial quality of his populist appeals for social justice.

Gore's courtship of North Carolina's Democratic organization later paid off handsomely. Similar efforts were rewarded in Georgia when Senator Nunn and Governor Joe Frank Harris announced in the closing days before the primary that they would cast their votes for Gore. Gore also benefited from the fact that broadcast stations in Tennessee which regularly covered the senator sent their signals into adjoining areas of Arkansas, Missouri, Mississippi, Alabama, Georgia, North Carolina, Virginia, and Kentucky.

Bruce Lightner, the Jackson coordinator for North Carolina, had also been active four years before. His recollections of 1984 induced him to insist on a more orderly game plan this time around, with clearer lines of authority and a specific timetable. Unlike his counterpart across the state line to the North, Lightner was already at work targeting the congressional districts where a good minority turnout (Native Americans were part of the constituency)—aided and abetted by mailings, fund-raisers and squads for taking voters to the polls—could elect Jackson delegates on Super Tuesday. He said he believed it was possible this time for Jackson to win the state if enough funds could be allocated to radio and television advertising. A white woman, Vee Stephenson, served as office manager, with her desk front and center to symbolize the outreach to all comers.

As he was doing in Iowa, Jackson sought out white audiences in the South to emphasize the multiracial quality of his populist appeals for social justice "on the front side of life" instead of welfare and prison "on the back side of life." Of all the candidates in the field, Jackson seemed to have the surest instinct for generating free media coverage of his activities, making up for a paucity of funds and the absence of media experts, pollsters, and campaign technicians from his entourage. He had no equal among other candidates in firing up a crowd. Young people, especially students, saw him as a fellow protester against the Old Order. Women responded to his emphasis on children, education, and family care. The elderly and disadvantaged identified with his compassion. Among African-Americans, their pride in Jesse Jackson's belief that the time had arrived for a black president of the United States of America was apparent everywhere, but in the South it radiated with a special poignancy. The voting returns on Super Tuesday would be one measure of the reality of that dream.

4

The Media and
the Political Process

The 1988 political campaign was the first in over 30 years to start with a wide-open race in both parties. At the outset, five Republicans and eight Democrats chose to enter the lists and at least three others in the latter party were mentioned as possible choices in the event of a brokered convention. Furthermore, a record high number of caucuses and primaries were scheduled. The sheer breadth of the election story with so many candidates running in so many places posed a logistical problem for national newspapers, wire services, and broadcast news organizations trying to provide adequate coverage.

The strain was compounded by economic limitations. The three major networks, all under new corporate management, had made stringent cutbacks in budget and personnel. The stock market crash in October 1987 had further softened advertising expenditures in both print and broadcast outlets. Caught in a vise between reduced resources and an expanded field of political combat, the media looked for new ways to organize their coverage. The practice of assigning correspondents one-on-one to each candidate or to make investigations in depth of every primary state was a luxury

---

thought to be no longer affordable.

The situation within the Democratic field was not entirely unfavorable to the candidacy of Jesse Jackson. Former senator Gary Hart of Colorado, the Democratic front-runner in the early polls, withdrew in 1987 after media exposés concerning his private life. This reduced the Democratic field to a relatively untried lot, dubbed "the seven dwarfs" by media pundits. An outsider by dint of race and lack of political experience, Jackson was nevertheless running for president a second time against a group of Democratic candidates relatively unknown on the national scene. Jackson's initial name recognition among voters, considered vital to waging a successful campaign, was substantially higher than that of the state governors and congressional officeholders also seeking the nomination. At the same time, he also started out as the most controversial candidate, scoring almost as many negatives as positives with voters canvassed by public opinion polls.

> The press lumped together the two reverends—Jackson and Pat Robertson—as the "preacher candidates," somehow less legitimate than the rest of the field.

The lengthy and complex process by which Americans pick their presidential candidates—including caucuses, primaries, and then a sometimes raucous national convention—is incomprehensible to foreigners and makes little sense to a lot of Americans. Even the experiment in 1988 to hold a regional primary on the same day in 14 Southern and border states was clouded by the fact that in all but three of those states Democrats and Republicans were permitted to cross over into each other's contests. Just two states, Arkansas and Mississippi, chose nominees for statewide office simultaneously with their presidential primaries, and it is significant that turnout of registered voters

32

was highest (48 percent) in Arkansas.

Sensitive to criticism after previous presidential elections, some leading media organizations altered their approach to political coverage. Long before the turn of the year, *The Washington Post* began defining slices of the electorate worth watching (baby boomers, evangelicals, blue collars in the Rust Belt, Yankees gone South) and fielded its staff to probe focus groups long before the candidates arrived. *The New York Times* rotated reporters covering particular candidates from time to time to broaden their perspective. The MacNeil-Lehrer show broadcast the basic stump speech delivered by each candidate, and the *Times* published the full texts. The major networks deployed their producers and correspondents into "zone coverage" of the political scene, picking up individual candidates as they converged on common issues rather than providing full-scale, one-on-one coverage of each contender.

Jackson's press secretary in his 1984 campaign was a long-time associate, Frank Watkins, an ordained minister with no journalistic experience. Watkins admitted that he disliked both the job and the press, and Jackson, who was ambivalent himself about white correspondents, was not one to delegate relations with the media. The 1988 campaign started with Watkins nominally still in charge, and it was not until the end of January that he was replaced by Elizabeth O. Colton, a white woman who had worked for *Newsweek* and National Public Radio. Most of Colton's experience had been overseas. She never enjoyed the personal access so vital to a political press secretary, and she eventually left the campaign and wrote *The Jackson Phenomenon*, an unflattering account of the candidate's relations with his staff.

The Jackson headquarters was moved from Washington to Jackson's base in Chicago, not a media crossroads. Political attention was focused first on Iowa, then on New Hampshire where Jackson was not a serious factor. An estimated 3,000 representatives of the media assembled in Iowa to cover the lightly attended caucuses there in January, but they concentrated on the presumed big hitters—Dole, Bush, Gephardt, and Simon. In its stereotyping fashion, the press lumped together the two reverends—Jackson and Pat Robertson—as the "preacher candidates," somehow less legitimate than the rest of the field. Jackson's habit of delivering five or six speeches a day, mostly repetitive, was not conducive to "making news," and his chronic lateness upset press deadlines. Such considerations contributed to Jackson's relative obscurity in accounts of a political process which the media struggled to get a handle on as the pack moved on to New Hampshire in February.

Newsweeklies, which for years traded on their colorful writing and superior research, are particularly susceptible to the ups and downs of candidates' fortunes. The difficulty of editing a news magazine during the primary season is that weeklies go to press just before the voting begins, with stories that are exposed to sometimes embarrassing public view for a week after unexpected results are official. Attempts to synthesize a more lasting idea—such as Newsweek's cover story on George Bush's "Wimp Factor"—can come back to haunt.

With only eight days between the voting in Iowa and New Hampshire, the editing challenge was particularly dicey. After Iowa, both Time and Newsweek could not resist the temptation to try to create the illusion of being on top of the news while carefully hedging the stories inside. Both featured bright yellow billboards on their covers—"Dole On A Roll" and "Dole Comes On Strong," respectively. When the editions hit the stands, the Dole momentum had been stopped cold in New Hampshire. U.S. News & World Report solved the dilemma by putting Pat Robertson on its cover in the wake of his surprise second-place finish in Iowa. Its cover story skirted the possibility that New Hampshire "might produce a third- or fourth-place finish" for Robertson (he actually came in fifth), projecting the story toward Super Tuesday in the South where it now predicted that Robertson's "invisible army" would be at its strongest.

On Super Tuesday Robertson's army turned out to be all but invisible. *The New Republic*, a journal of opinion, was free to exercise its preference for publisher Martin Peretz's former student at Harvard, Albert Gore, Jr., with an endorsement and Gore's picture on the cover in the issue dated March 7, the day before Super Tuesday.

The Jackson Advantage

The decay of party loyalties and party organizations had thrown open the nominating process to the politics of self-starters, individuals who put themselves forward with their own personal staffs, consultants, and campaign strategies. Experienced in the politics of protest, including the art of attracting media attention to a cause, Jackson could use his genius for publicity to try to compensate for campaign disorganization and a lack of funds in a process in which million-dollar budgets for television ads had become the single most important ingredient of presidential campaigning.

"Negative advertising" had proved to be an unpleasant but effective part of electioneering, and 1988 was to produce a banner crop of attack television ads. Early on, Gephardt trashed Dukakis among Midwestern farmers by making fun of a remark by the Massachusetts governor that they might consider raising Belgian endive as a new cash crop suited to the food tastes of a new generation. Dukakis fought back by denouncing Gephardt's "protectionist" views on trade policies. Jackson, who was not considered by his rivals as a serious threat at the time, remained outside the line of fire. Since the eventual nominee would have to build a winning coalition without antagonizing African-Americans or other pro-civil rights voters, no candidate wanted to be perceived as attacking Jackson because of his race. Thus, his critics began complaining about the "free ride" Jackson was getting from both his rivals and the press.

In the televised debates which became a staple of the winnowing-out process, Jackson seized for himself the role of

35

positive mediator between his warring rivals. He scrupulously avoided criticizing his Democratic opponents on these programs. Often he urged them to get together and concentrate on the Republicans. He employed his own considerable debating skills with punchy sound-bites, skewering the G.O.P. on issues which the handlers surrounding his cautious rivals judged to be too risky.

> The notion that Jackson was receiving a free ride from the media was countered by the findings of FAIR, which concluded that "Jackson has been running against the press every step of the way."

The Center for Media and Public Affairs in Washington, D.C., monitored election stories on the ABC, CBS, and NBC evening news shows from January 1 until the week after Super Tuesday. Statements on each candidate's character, job performance, and issue stands were counted as being either positive or negative. Jackson's share of the Democrats' coverage nearly tripled (from 8 percent to 21 percent of the total) during the weeks of the Super Tuesday campaign from what it had been prior to the New Hampshire primary. Positive mentions comprised 74 percent of Jackson's network total, compared with 50 percent for Gore and 40 percent each for Dukakis and Gephardt. In the week after Super Tuesday, Jackson's image score soared to 100 percent favorable mentions versus 43 percent each for Dukakis and Gore.

The notion that Jackson was receiving a free ride from the media as well as from his political rivals was countered, however, by findings assembled by FAIR (Fairness & Accuracy In Reporting), based in New York and Washington, citing stories in the *Wall Street Journal*, *The Washington Post*, *The New York Times*, *Newsweek*, and other print media which tended to dismiss Jackson as a serious contender for the presidency. Moreover, these news organizations reprised his "Hymietown" remarks of four years before, dwelled on his past relationships with Louis Farrakhan and Yasir Arafat, criticized his handling of the finances of Operation PUSH, and charged that his policies were to the left of mainstream American politics. FAIR concluded that "Jackson has been running against the press every step of the way."

If it was broadly true that Jackson fared better on television than in the pages of the print media, television coverage, with its emphasis on photo opportunities, was made-to-order for a colorful and charismatic individual like Jackson, especially in contrast to other candidates variously described as aloof, wooden, or pompous. His well-honed rhetoric on pocketbook issues and the day-to-day needs of ordinary folk might have afforded him an additional advantage except that network television news, according to surveys published in *USA Today* during the January-March primary period, never devoted more than 20 percent of their broadcast time to substantive issues while spending 80 percent of their time on campaign attacks, candidate mistakes, and "horse-race" reports on who was ahead in the polls.

In this front-loaded system, Jackson (along with Gore) was pretty well engulfed by stories centering on the poll leaders: Gephardt, Simon, and Dukakis among the Democrats, Bush and Dole among the Republicans. Jackson's showing (8.8 percent in Iowa and 7.8 percent in New Hampshire) was not calculated to make banner headlines.

Covering Super Tuesday

Robertson's second-place finish in the Republican Iowa caucuses took both the pollsters and the press by surprise, and the Gallup poll, in a special survey for a group of television clients, mistakenly predicted a Dole win in New Hampshire. Such errors, when focusing on only one state at a time, made the challenge of trying to cover Super Tuesday all the more problematic. The geographical expanse from

Maryland to Florida to Texas was far too vast for candidates to canvass personally or for the national media to cover thoroughly. Now that it was the turn of Gore and Jackson to enjoy the status of native sons, media attention became fragmented and dispersed.

Jackson took advantage of his chartered plane to drop into several local media markets per day, logging free time on news broadcasts, even when not receiving much attention on the networks or in prestigious newspapers in Washington, New York, Los Angeles, Boston, Chicago, or Philadelphia. Based on past experience, he concentrated on radio stations, including black programs, all over the South, which traveling correspondents never had time to monitor. He could do several broadcasts in one sitting from his hotel room by telephone.

His chief rivals, Gore and Dukakis, traveled with a full entourage of issue and media advisers, while Jackson hammered away at his basic theme: "Save the family, save family farms, save jobs, save the environment, keep drugs out, keep jobs in, reinvest in America, down with drugs, up with hope. We, the people, will win." Jackson, who had made a career of going into schools talking about drug abuse, emphasized his solutions to the drug problem from the very outset of his campaign, forcing other candidates to address the issue. His vision of the New South, he emphasized, was for black and white to find "common ground" to end the "economic violence" which still lingered behind the facade of improved civil rights.

In some states (such as Alabama and Maryland), Democratic party officials complained that their primaries were being ignored as the media zeroed in on the big delegate prizes such as Florida and Texas. Television debates between the candidates, which took place in Texas, Virginia, and Georgia, were restricted to Cable News Network or the Public Broadcasting Service and were not picked up by many limited-audience stations or else were scheduled at off-hours. Candidates hopscotched over the territory from tarmac to television studio. After announcing a full evening of prime-time devoted to the Super Tuesday primary results, the networks scaled back to an hour or less and went off the air before the returns were even complete.

Regional newspapers were more thorough, although reporters and editors were skeptical over how many in the audience really cared. Jesse Jackson might have warranted being treated as a "favorite son" in the South, but it was Senator Gore, who was closest to state Democratic leaders, who had the ear of political reporters. The *Atlanta Constitution-Journal* went all out before and during the Super Tuesday campaign period with special sections on the issues, profiles of each candidate, and regional polls conducted by the Roper Organization. Editor Bill Kovach ruefully told a media conference in January, however, that the papers would probably have to repeat many of their stories as Super Tuesday drew nearer. On the weekend before the voting, the *Constitution* distributed a special 28-page insert in its Sunday edition providing a detailed guide on issues and candidates and primary races throughout the South. The voter turnout in Georgia hit 40 percent, among the highest. In North Carolina, the *Charlotte Observer* provided in-depth coverage of the closely contested Tarheel State but turnout there (31 percent) was disappointing.

Cable News Network, based in Atlanta, inaugurated a nightly dinner-time half-hour, "Politics 88," in January when, co-anchor Mary Alice Williams conceded, "the audience didn't give a damn." Taking advantage of the ability of cable to cater to specialized audiences, CNN tailored its coverage to political aficionados as the campaign heated up. Bernard Shaw, the show's other co-anchor, brought a cool calm to his commentary, in sharp contrast to the high-decibel style of CBS's Dan Rather, ABC's Sam Donaldson, and NBC's Chris Wallace. (It was Shaw who later blew Michael Dukakis out of the water during a television debate with Bush with his deadpan question about what the Democratic nominee would do if his wife were the victim of a rapist.)

Former network correspondent Marvin Kalb, now a professor at Harvard, conducted hour-long interviews over the Public Broadcasting Service with each presidential hopeful (only George Bush refused his invitation). The highest rating was achieved by the program with Gary Hart, after the latter re-entered the race.

Many editors were less than enthusiastic about the Super Tuesday experiment. Ferrel Guillory, columnist and editorial writer for the *Raleigh News & Observer* in North Carolina, wrote on January 8, 1988: "There is something wrong with a nominating process that gives one state the loudest voice and then produces candidates who cannot even carry that state. There is something wrong, too, with a nominating process that permits a Super Tuesday (in March) . . . when 20 states—14 in the South—will select a third of the delegates to the Republican and Democratic conventions. Such 'front-loading' of the selection process amounts to a rush-to-judgment. It sets up a furious airport-to-airport campaign over a wide swath of the country—too much ground to cover with little time for reflection on the part of both candidates and voters."

Local television stations, however, thanks to the ability to use mobile vans and satellites, deployed correspondents to areas formerly covered exclusively by networks. Sometimes local personnel lacked the political experience and expertise of network veterans, but their reports lent the nightly news an immediacy and relevance which might have been expected to increase viewer interest in Super Tuesday. A possible contrary effect has been suggested by analysts who argue that the glut of information has so surfeited bewildered viewers that they tend to tune out or discount political news that is not simple and dramatic.

Technological change has also had an impact on campaign coverage by the print media. Dissemination by computer increased the ability of local newsrooms to keep abreast of the daily flow of political information almost simultaneously with its happening. Lap-top word processors for instant transmission of stories from campaign press stops have become as standard as satellite transmission of television tape. These wonders of technology, however, work against writers who file an off-beat account or an in-depth examination that flies in the face of conventional wisdom. Editors and producers are not only looking over the shoulders of the reporters in the field but keeping abreast of the competition on their monitors. For a political writer, going out on a limb in such situations was living dangerously. Too many stories about Jackson were likely to draw frowns from the home office when he was not considered to be part of the big picture.

One of the popular innovations launched in time for the 1988 primaries was a computerized service, sold under the name Campaign Hot Line, to promote an eventually more substantial data base, searchable by computer and available to businesses, lobbyists, trade organizations, libraries, and universities. Founded by a pair of former political consultants and based in low-overhead offices in the Virginia suburbs outside Washington, Hot Line provided a daily digest of newspaper stories, television reports, campaign schedules, and instant analysis by a panel of political consultants from both major parties. Clipping newspapers available at dawn each morning in Washington, D.C., and monitoring late-night and early-morning news telecasts, a bright but modestly paid crew of young editorial assistants also assembled 200 words straight from the press secretaries of each of the major candidates (it took Jackson's press headquarters several weeks to catch on to the possibilities). With a good eye for trendy ideas and the instant quote, Hot Line offered a daily smorgasbord of political fare ready to be downloaded in 10 minutes at 10:00 a.m. every day by newspaper and broadcast subscribers. As part of the deal, subscribers made their own lead political stories available to Hot Line news central simultaneously with publication in exchange for a discount.

Hot Line printouts were on the desks of reporters and

41

editors whom I visited throughout the South in the weeks before Super Tuesday. *The Washington Post* distributed 20 copies around the office every day and forwarded the contents to correspondents in the boondocks. Andy Mollison, based in the Washington bureau of the *Atlanta Constitution*, said he never could have caught up with the political beat without it. He described the service as a "fantastic tip sheet for story ideas you can follow up on your own." Campaign managers, without exception, took advantage of the opportunity to put their own instant spin on the outcome of television debates or primary elections.

The worry that such devices increase tendencies toward herd reporting and Eastern seaboard influence is mitigated by the argument that papers and broadcast outlets in the provinces were provided with a showcase within established power centers. Hot Line probably quickened the pace by which campaign theories spread in the press (e.g., "Gephardt faltering" just before Iowa voters proved otherwise; "Dole on a roll" before stubbing his toe in New Hampshire; and "What does Jesse want?").

Doug Bailey, a Republican consultant before becoming Hot Line co-editor with former Democratic consultant Ron Rosenblith, made no apologies for the lack of journalistic experience among Hot Line's working staff. "Most reporters don't really understand politics," he said. "The professional press sometimes cannot separate titillation from real news. Any political consultant could have told you that Gary Hart wasn't politically viable."

Polls

Although more useful for identifying current patterns of attitudes and beliefs than predicting future behavior, polls have become a staple of political coverage. Whether such knowledge disseminated by the mass media during an election infringes on the process itself is much debated. But the fact remains that the publication of poll results was one of the staples of reportage of the 1988 election from beginning to end. Jackson was an early beneficiary of polls because his name recognition was much higher at the outset than the other Democrats'. In the CBS-*New York Times* survey conducted in November 1987, Jackson led the trial heat among likely Democratic primary voters with 25 percent, compared to Paul Simon at 10 and Michael Dukakis at nine. Of course, 14 percent said they were still undecided.

The evolution of scientific polling has presented political reporters with an expanded source of inside information. At first reporters tended to demean pollsters as academic upstarts encroaching upon their professional turf. They have now learned how to have the best of both worlds. Looking for a handle on the elections, they habitually sneak the latest poll results into their pre-election leads. If the poll forecasts prove wrong, they write about "upsets" while blaming the pollsters for misleading the public.

Pollsters have a special fear and loathing for primaries. In the first place, the number of voters who actually exercise their franchise in a party primary election is usually only a minority of those eligible, so the pollster can never be sure that the people being interviewed will be the same ones who show up at the polls. In primaries where voters are restricted to selecting among candidates of their registered party, the choices tend to be volatile because it is psychologically easier to shift allegiances from one candidate to the next within the same political family. Much more than in two-party elections, voters wait until the last minute to make up their minds. Where voters are free to participate in party primaries without belonging to that party in advance, pollsters cannot be sure which contest they will choose. Closet Republicans will cast a vote in a Democratic primary to achieve some tactical advantage for their side, or vice versa.

Since many primaries occur early in the political season, candidates have not always had a chance to establish their political identity and voters have not yet focused on the political race. Polls taken in the months well ahead of the actual voting are usually mush: the numbers reflect little more than the fleeting recognition of names in the news. This makes for drastic swings when undecided voters begin making up their minds or changing in response to un-anticipated events. Since a poll is only a snapshot of conditions at the instant the questions are asked of a poten-tial voter, that picture may be outdated even before the statistics are analyzed, and even more stale when they are distributed for publication. Added to all these are the inaccuracies generated by sampling error, questionnaire phrasing, and interviewer bias. Despite such problems, public opinion polling is a useful reporting device when evaluated properly.

The *Atlanta Constitution*, as part of its specialized cover-age of Super Tuesday, hired the Roper Organization to conduct a series of telephone polls in 12 Southern states. An original sample of 15,354 respondents was reduced to 7,689 who said they were "pretty sure" to vote on March 8. The calls were made using random samples of both listed and unlisted phone numbers in a representative cross-section of telephone exchanges. Despite these precautions, the re-sults announced in the Sunday paper before the primaries placed Jackson and Dukakis first and second and underes-timated Gore's actual vote by nearly 10 points. The survey had been conducted from February 19 through February 27—two to three weeks before the voting. A smaller survey during the last weekend before the voting and published on primary day—interviewing as few as 830 likely Democratic voters—showed slight gains by Dukakis and Gore but a surge toward Jackson with increased margins over his two leading opponents. In the event, it turned out that it was Gore who was surging. Such overall figures, in any case, were meaningless in the race for delegates being decided by results in each congressional district across the South. Poll-ing at that level, however, would have been prohibitively expensive. That did not prevent widespread dissemination of the *Constitution*'s findings within candidates' campaign organizations as well as in other newspapers and broadcasting outlets. No one has ever succeeded, however, in accurately measuring the effect of such information on the voting electorate or in determining whether voters really like to jump on a bandwagon or, conversely, throw their support to an underdog.

The Roper Organization fared better in its examination of candidate standings on a state-by-state basis, correctly reporting that Dukakis was carrying the key states, Texas and Florida, and that Jackson would do well in Mississippi, Alabama, Georgia, South Carolina, and Virginia. Jackson was reported, however, as being nine points ahead of Gore in North Carolina, although Gore eventually won the state, with Dukakis in third place. Dukakis was also running second to Jackson (though 20 points behind) in the *Constitution*'s home state of Georgia. Gore was in fourth place, trailing even Gephardt. He finished nearly 17 points ahead of Dukakis in the Georgia primary and less than 10 behind Jackson. The perils of a small sample gathered well in advance of the voting were illustrated when Dukakis was shown to be in a dead heat with Jackson in Louisiana. On Super Tuesday Jackson carried the state by seven points over Gore, with Dukakis 13 points behind the latter.

The volatility of primary polls is further documented by the fact that Gary Hart was ahead in five Super Tuesday states polled by Roper in January 1988. Mason-Dixon Opinion Research, a firm hired by a number of Southern newspapers and broadcast stations, reported Hart ahead in Texas and Florida in January and second in 10 other Super Tuesday states. Hart led nationwide in January polls by Gallup, CBS, and NBC. An ABC-*Washington Post* poll that month showed Jackson leading Hart 25 percent to 23 percent. Of course, nearly half of those interviewed at this stage had no opinion to express on Democratic presidential candidates. The January poll in the *Constitution* showed Jackson at 24 percent, Hart 20, Gore 18, and Dukakis seven. The Scripps-Howard News Service put Jackson at 26 percent, Hart 20, Gore 12, and

45

Dukakis nine.

An interesting feature of all this data is that Jesse Jackson's strength among Super Tuesday voters varied only slightly within statistical margins of error during January and February. About one in four preferred Jackson before, during and after the Super Tuesday campaign. One clue to the reason for this was provided in a survey undertaken for the Democratic Leadership Council in October 1987, before and after a televised debate among the candidates on national security issues. The DLC chose pollster Stanley Greenberg to interview voters in Atlanta, Jacksonville (Florida), and Charlotte (North Carolina), who had voted for Ronald Reagan in 1984 and also for the winning Democratic candidate for U.S. senator from those states in 1986.

According to the report prepared by Greenberg's Analysis Group, titled "The National Security Debate Survey," 91 percent of these swing voters (87 percent whites) felt they knew enough about Jackson to express an opinion about him compared to less than 50 percent for any of the others. They went into the debate with 43 percent expressing positive feelings about him and 48 percent negative. After the debate, Jackson's rating improved to 48 percent positive versus 45 percent negative, but the figures showed he had the least room to shape his image. It was at this debate that Gore staked out a position favoring a large military budget, a strong presence in the Persian Gulf, and continued support for the Contras in Central America. Favorable impressions of Gore rose from 30 percent before the debate to 69 percent afterwards. At the same time, unfavorable impressions rose from only 17 percent to 19. Dukakis rose from 28 percent positive to 51 percent, but unfavorable impressions also soared from 18 percent to 31 percent.

The Gore potential for improvement among these largely white swing voters was clearly evident. His problem was that 37 percent of those interviewed said they planned to vote in the Republican primary, nearly as many as the 45 percent who said they would participate in the Democratic contest on Super Tuesday. Jackson's support among these mostly white voters who said they would vote in the Democratic primary dropped from 23 percent before the debate to 9 percent after the other candidates became better known and liked.

An interesting aspect of the DLC poll, as well as some of the issue questions in the *Atlanta Constitution*-Roper poll, were the insights they provided about eligible voters in the Super Tuesday primary. The voters who had backed Reagan in 1984 and a Democrat in 1986 described themselves as more "moderate" than "conservative." Forty percent described themselves as Democrats, 37 percent as Republicans, and 19 percent as independents. The division between men and women was the same as that for the general population. Twenty-two percent were under 30 years old, 37 percent between the ages of 30 and 45, and 18 percent over 60.

As a group, according to Greenberg's report, they had "substantial doubts about Democrats on questions of national strength and national defense" and "questioned the Democrats on ensuring the country's economic prosperity. They believe that the Democrats in the past have lost touch with working people in favor of special interests and they are uncertain whether the Democrats have started out in a different direction."

As for the Republicans, "these Southern swing voters, by their own accounts, were drawn to Ronald Reagan (64 percent) rather than repelled by Walter Mondale (26 percent). . . . They are critical of the Republicans and Ronald Reagan in two principal areas: providing for kids and their future opportunities and investing in America to make her competitive and strong."

In its survey of the broader electorate, the *Atlanta Constitution*-Roper poll (as reported by Dwight L. Morris in "The Polling Report," Oct. 26, 1987) "found a fairly broad consensus on the importance of a variety of domestic and foreign policy issues . . . . However, beneath the surface of this apparent consensus, the survey reveals considerable division in Southern society. There is not one South but many Souths—a black South and a white South, a male South and a female South, an 'old' South and a 'new' South . . . . Like the rest of the country the South is made up of groups that bring to politics all kinds of agendas."

The four issues at the top of the list of concerns among all Roper poll respondents combined were drug abuse (82 percent), education (81 percent), Social Security (73 percent), and taxes (68 percent). At the bottom were aid to the Contras (39 percent), inflation (48 percent), catastrophic illness insurance (49 percent), and abortion (49 percent). Such issue lists in response to pollsters' questions do not reveal which are politically salient, that is, important enough to make a voter switch a vote from one party or candidate to another. Political consultants focus on data which will identify switchers, even though the issue, such as abortion, may not top the list with the most mentions in a general quiz. Jackson hoped to switch voters who might not ordinarily vote for an African-American candidate—white rural farmers or Republican women in the suburbs—by taking strong positions on policies that touched them deeply.

By breaking out the subgroups on each issue, however, the existence of a non-monolithic South was well documented by Roper. For example, on the issue of unemployment, 80 percent of African-Americans interviewed said they were "very concerned" about the problem as against only 50 percent among whites. Among native Southerners, 60 percent said they were "very concerned," as against only 42 percent of those who had lived in the South for less than 10 years.

Eighty-three percent of African-Americans said they were worried about Social Security versus 70 percent among whites and 64 percent among newcomers of both races. Interestingly, 67 percent of African-Americans said they felt concern on the school-prayer issue versus 56 percent among whites.

Seventy percent of the women interviewed showed concern for the homeless, 10 points higher than men.

Dial-a-Quote

Academic writers on politics are enjoying a vogue among the new breed of political journalists searching for deeper meanings to explain breaking news. Professor Hugh Winebrenner of Drake University in Des Moines, author of *The Iowa Precinct Caucuses: Making of a Media Event* and a sharp critic of the caucuses, became a source sought by visiting correspondents nearly as much as the *Des Moines Register and Tribune*'s veteran political writer, David Yepsen. Ethel Klein, a professor at Columbia University and author of *The Gender Gap*, found her surveys on women's attitudes in politics the object of frequent phone calls from the media.

Professor Larry Sabato at the University of Virginia, the author of several works on Virginia and national politics, said that his phone traffic picked up considerably as Super Tuesday approached. Twin brothers Earl and Merle Black, teaching at the universities of South and North Carolina respectively, wrote the "must" book for reporters examining trends below the Mason-Dixon line, *Politics and Society in the South*. Brother Merle from Chapel Hill was a featured speaker at the Super Tuesday Summit held by the Democratic Leadership Council in Atlanta in June 1987. One of the premises of the book is that the Democrats cannot win the South for their nominee until they can appeal to the region's expanding white middle class. By January 1988, his Chapel Hill phone log showed he had received 200 calls from papers in Boston, Chicago, Washington, Atlanta, and San Francisco, not to mention the cable and broadcast networks. At press headquarters in Columbia, South Carolina, on the night of the Republican primary in that state, brother Earl spent the evening doing stand-up television interviews and holding court with the media biggies. (At the open Democratic precinct caucuses in Columbia a week later he stood with

> **"Anybody who thinks the press is too powerful should look at my campaign," said Bruce Babbitt. "I got great coverage, but it did me little good with the voters."**

voters backing Gore.)

Professor James David Barber of Duke University in Durham, North Carolina, author of books on presidential character, was in demand for op-ed pieces after the Gary Hart affair. He expressed a low opinion of the present system for nominating presidents, including Super Tuesday. "Grand opera behind a banal facade," he said. His preference was for a procedure which would restore the peer review which used to take place at national conventions and which is the system by which parliamentary democracies such as Britain choose their political leaders. A popular primary might be used to decide between the leading choices of the insiders. In Barber's opinion, Gore wasn't ready for the presidency and Jesse Jackson was "in no way qualified." Meanwhile, he thought, it was up to the media to show that politics could be covered in more depth, candidate biographies probed more stringently, and the whole style of campaign reporting devoted "to make reality interesting." As it is, television campaign coverage contains "too much inside baseball" and print reporting is too full of dull detail which "nobody reads except the reporter's mother."

A Loser Appraises the Media

One of the first dropouts in the so-called winnowing primary process was former governor Bruce Babbitt of Arizona, who, like Adlai Stevenson in 1952 and 1956, turned out to be more popular among the working press than the voters. Quoted in *The Washington Post* after his withdrawal from the race in February, Babbitt praised the "retail politics" in the early states as a learning experience for newcomers. He said a long campaign is necessary to develop leaders when there is no parliamentary system for such apprenticeship. As for the media: "The notion that the media don't cover politics is ridiculous. I mean, every time a candidate gives off even a shred of evidence that he has something to say, it gets reported. The reason that issues don't get reported is that candidates aren't talking about them. The press does tend to run as a pack, however. There's a tendency to pile on when you're down and float you into the stratosphere when you're up. This exaggerates the normal ups and downs of a campaign. It turns a bumpy ride into a roller coaster. But anybody who thinks the press is too powerful should look at my campaign. I got great coverage, but it did me little good with the voters."

Conventional wisdom was that Babbitt never recovered from the strange facial mannerisms he exhibited on the earliest televised candidate debates. Similarly, Jesse Jackson was faulted for a South Carolina accent which sometimes made his fast spoken words unintelligible to unattuned ears. Michael Dukakis, of course, came over the tube as too un-emotional and aloof. Al Gore was accused of being too glib. In the Information Age such factors can be crucial.

5

The Road to
Super Tuesday

Jesse Jackson started his quest for Super Tuesday delegates with one significant advantage: he had never really stopped campaigning after his first run in 1984 and, of course, he had been an active participant in Southern affairs since the civil rights movement in the sixties. His name recognition in the South and border states was high. He knew the turf better than any of his opponents, all of them newcomers to the national stage.

One of the very first priorities of his national campaign staff, organized under the direction of Gerald Austin, a white veteran of successful political campaigns in Ohio, was the leasing of an airplane, ready to transport Jackson at a moment's notice to take advantage of opportunities from Texas to Maryland. Although lacking funds to hire a large staff of polling and media advertising experts, Jackson had proved himself a past master at obtaining "free media."

A Jackson foray was usually accompanied by a high-energy display of pressing the flesh and firsthand contact with the crowds swarming around him upon his arrival. Stops on his campaign itinerary were often scheduled on the spur of the moment. At least one campaign organizer along the hectic trail was heard to say, "Glad to see Jesse come. Glad to see him go."

From the very start of the campaign it was clear that a special relationship bound Jesse Jackson with his supporters. At rallies, the intensity of the audience response to his ideas was qualitatively different from that evoked by other candidates. African-Americans often replied as if in church "Tell it, Jesse," "That's right!" picking up the rhythm of Jackson's appeals to keep hope alive. Whites, though sometimes awkwardly, were caught up in the occasion, echoing the refrain from their brothers and sisters of color. The basic Jackson speech, later reprised dramatically over television at the Democratic national convention in Atlanta, sparked an emotional response like nothing else I have witnessed in 50 years of participating in and reporting politics. "Invest in the front side of life instead of spending on the back side of life." "I was the child of a teenage mother; my grandmother was only 13 when she gave birth. I was born in the slum, but the slum was not born in me. If I can get out, you can get out."

Only Pat Robertson's evangelical appeals approached the Jackson phenomenon, but the crowds were smaller and the message more of a negative assault on the non-believers. Robertson's followers tended to be tight-lipped, suspicious of outsiders, and isolated from the rest of the secular world, though outwardly they did not look any different from the white husbands, wives, and children one saw in any Southern city, town, or hamlet. Jackson enthusiasts, on the other hand, were eager to share their feelings and convictions even with strangers, explaining why the time had come for Presi-

> The basic Jackson speech, later reprised at the national convention, sparked an emotional response like nothing else I have witnessed in 50 years of reporting politics.

54

dent Jesse. The old, young, poor, and prosperous were drawn together by pride in this extraordinary political movement, one that most had never imagined to be possible in their lifetime.

Most of all, one was struck by the children. Whether clinging to their parents or shouting their replies to the candidate's exhortations, "Down with dope, up with hope! I am somebody!" a special look on their faces bordered on ecstasy. Men and women alike rushed to shake Jackson's hand as he reached out to the throngs lining the paths forged by the traveling media and Secret Service. Jackson rarely missed the opportunity to pick up a small child in his arms, smiling broadly and endeavoring, not always with success, to persuade the youngster to join him in a thumbs-up gesture of optimism. Then he would plant a kiss on the cheek and hand the child down to the arms of an adoring parent.

Jackson's message—the need for good jobs, better schools, and improved health care—was couched in terms independent of race. During the television debates between the full slate of candidates, it was Jackson who sought to cool down the exchange of barbs between his fellow Democrats. Rivals complained that Jackson was being given a "pass" by the media critics, fearful of appearing prejudiced. Jackson supporters, on the other hand, complained of slights by the local press in the South. Lacking funds for get-out-the-vote mailings or television ads, Jackson was his own cheerleader.

Jackson: "What's happening March 8?"
Crowd: "Super Tuesday."
Jackson: "And what are you going to do?"
Crowd: "Vote."
Jackson: "And who are you going to vote for?"
Crowd: "Jesse Jackson!"

Michael Oreskes, reporting for *The New York Times*, observed: "It is difficult to imagine Governor Michael S. Dukakis, Representative Richard A. Gephardt, or Senator Albert Gore, Jr., invoking this incantation or churning these emotions."

The Jackson campaign for Super Tuesday, however, was beset by a number of problems, some but not all endemic to the hectic character of presidential primaries. Jackson's main headquarters in Chicago was not always in close communication with organizers in the field, and Jackson, on the road most of the time, had a penchant for private telephone calls that others in the campaign were not privy to.

There was a natural rivalry between African-American politicians who had won their spurs earlier on the local scene and Jackson, suddenly projecting himself as a national leader.

"The people in the national campaign," remarked State Senator Mike Figures, a Jackson coordinator in Alabama, "always have their own ideas, their own judgments. They kept scheduling Jesse where he could talk to white voters. We might have used him better up in the Black Belt, bringing out the vote we already knew we had ... but you don't need that much of a structured campaign for someone like Jesse Jackson. The Jackson campaign is an extension of his own personality. Voters are attached to Jesse like kids are attached to Michael Jackson: charisma."

The money problem was ever-present. (It was only after the favorable results of Super Tuesday that contributions began to flow more freely.) Gore was able to mount a massive television blitz in the last days before the voting. Dukakis forces had the know-how and the wherewithal to rent a studio in Atlanta and offer satellite link-ups with local television stations all over the region that wanted a one-on-one interview between the candidate and their local anchors. The Dukakis campaign picked up the tab.

"I had told national we needed $500,000 for a television budget," said Bruce Lightner, Jackson's campaign coordinator in North Carolina. "We ended up spending $16,000 on four spots in Winston-Salem, Raleigh, Greensboro, and Charlotte. And we lost the state to Gore by 8,000 votes."

In 1984, according to Lightner, "the clergy had been crucial, especially for fund-raising. We had planned a Super Tuesday Sunday in February to raise money. People For the American Way (a nonprofit organization focused on the separation of church and state) put out a press release up in Washington raising questions about soliciting campaign contributions in church. That scared off about 85 percent of the preachers."

Clergymen and elected black officials were the core of the Jackson operation in the field. Unfortunately, neither category was free to devote full-time attention to the primary. Many of the state legislatures were in session during most of the run-up period to Super Tuesday and clergymen, of course, had parish duties to attend. Those individuals recruited as full-time staffers, like Billy Young in South Georgia, a veteran of 1984, were desperately overextended. Working out of Macon, Young was constantly on call as far away as Albany and Savannah, riding the circuit on hundreds of problems day after day with barely enough time to eat or sleep.

"Billy was one of my stars," said Georgia State Senator Gene Walker, Jackson co-chair in that state. "I'm 53 and I never met a person as naturally good and unpretentious, totally committed to the Rainbow concept. Billy was the main man in carrying the 8th Congressional District, one of six we targeted in Georgia. And we carried it."

The Jackson campaign in 1984 had contended with the fact that many black leaders in the South had committed to Walter Mondale. This time around there was more unity behind Jackson since none of his white rivals had a track record to compare with Mondale's. Although no one endorsed any of Jackson's opponents, there were important absentees from his effort. Mayor Andrew Young of Atlanta, Lieutenant Governor Douglas Wilder of Virginia, and Congressman Mike Espy of Mississippi maintained neutrality in the primary contests. There was a natural rivalry between African-American politicians who had won their spurs earlier on the local scene and Jackson, suddenly projecting himself as a national leader. The Jackson ego and personality did not always endear him to colleagues. Mayor Richard Arrington of Birmingham, who had backed Mondale in 1984, announced for Jackson this time around. Arrington, however, was traveling in Egypt when the voting began on Super Tuesday.

The New South Coalition, made up mostly of Alabama state legislators, and the Alabama Democratic Caucus, an African-American group that had backed Mondale in 1984, sometimes worked at cross purposes. Fred Gray, a Montgomery lawyer active in the caucus, explained that "we supported Mondale four years ago, because he was the clear front-runner and was more electable . . . . This time Jackson has matured. He is more broad-based. He is not strictly geared to a symbolic, personal showing . . . . We're a grass-roots organization. We have networks in over 60 counties. Since Jackson didn't have any street money, we relied on volunteers."

In Montgomery County, the New South Coalition and the Alabama Democratic Caucus each endorsed a different slate of delegates, both pledged to Jackson. The slate backed by the caucus won four spots; the New South Coalition none. The turnout of voters in Alabama was lower than four years before, but this time the presidential primary was split away from the contests for state office held on a later date.

In the waning days of the campaign in Louisiana, representatives from Jackson headquarters in Chicago clashed with local African-American Democrats charged with Super Tuesday responsibilities. Jackson failed to make the key election-eve party rally in North Carolina (he was stuck in Washington because the pilot of the campaign plane had already flown his FAA maximum for the day). The decision to spend primary night in Texas, where Jackson forces hoped to win, did not go down well with those organizing victory parties in states where success seemed more assured.

Such clashes were minor compared with the overall momentum of Jackson's extraordinary journey in presidential politics. "Jesse is forcing people to entertain the notion that a black man can be president," said Senator Walker. "It's a process. We can't lose. If not this time, next time. Look how long we had slavery. This is only Jesse's second try. He's a lot younger than Reagan." The white co-chair for Jackson in Georgia, Decatur's Mayor Michael Mears (whose city is 65 percent white), said: "I think my white constituents supported my involvement with the Jackson campaign, though they did not vote for him. I ran for re-election three weeks after I endorsed Jesse and received 85 percent of the vote.... If we didn't win acceptance among white voters this time, we won their tolerance. That's a plus for the future."

John T. Flannery, Jackson co-chair in Northern Virginia where Jackson's vote among whites reached double digits (23 percent in Fairfax County, which is only 7 percent black), said: "The Democratic network in the 10th Congressional District was reluctant at first. The issue-oriented people resisted. But they began listening to Jesse on the issues and they liked what they heard.

"On two days' notice we scheduled Jesse into George Mason University," Flannery continued. "It was in the middle of Fairfax County and provided a mostly white audience. There was a packed house of 900. . . . We picked up 50 volunteers after that rally. It got big media coverage, all affirmative. . . .

"Jackson's numbers far outreached the number of blacks in an area where people pay attention to government, pay attention to the policy issues, and are not hung up on the question of race. . . . Northern Virginia is the story of what is possible in America when voters focus on the issues."

The attraction of Jackson's positions on the issues, his inspiring performances on the stump, plus the democratic ideal that all persons should have an equal opportunity to hold the highest office in the land were powerful motivators for many black and white voters. But in the secrecy of the voting booth only a fraction of white voters, albeit a growing one, seemed ready in 1988 to implement the equal opportunity ideal.

Some white voters opposed Jesse Jackson because they disagreed with his positions or doubted his qualifications. Some argued on tactical grounds that while they might be willing to vote for a Democratic ticket headed by Jackson, they believed that the mass of the American people were not capable of rising above racism. Thus a primary vote for Jackson would be a wasted vote, according to this subtle form of applied prejudice. It is difficult to measure emotions which individuals want to hide from themselves as well as from others. But it would be foolish to ignore the reality that the virus of racism still infects the American body politic.

In the South on Super Tuesday the white Democratic establishment, with rare exceptions, threw its weight behind the candidacy of Senator Albert Gore. The regional newspapers, by and large, reflected the fact that their principal sources of political news were the same white elected officials who were doing their best to defeat Jackson.

Senator Walker said, "The *Atlanta Constitution* was a big disappointment to me. Ralph McGill used to write about the way the nation should be. The present *Constitution* wrote about what can't be done instead of what should be done. The *Constitution* assigned a white female reporter to write their main profile on Jesse Jackson. She would go around and talk to anybody who had something negative to say about Jesse. That became the gospel. . . . After the voting on Super Tuesday, whose picture was on the front page? Al Gore's. 'Gore Makes It 3-Man Democratic Race,' the *Constitution* headline went. 'South has its say: Gore, Bush Like What They Hear.' Jesse had earned the right to be on the front page of the paper. He got 40 percent in Georgia to Gore's 32 percent. . . . They gave the play to the man they hoped would win."

6

At the Polls

It is a truism that elections are decided at the precinct level, but in all the hoopla of media politics the reality of the voting booth is often eclipsed. A worm's-eye view of Super Tuesday from the actual polling place—on primary day in Georgia and on caucus day in South Carolina—confirmed the fact that Jackson voters, overwhelmingly black, and supporters of other candidates, overwhelmingly white, marched to different drumbeats.

The word "marched" is used advisedly, because in spite of all the investments in door-to-door campaigning, telephone canvasses, and car pools, most of those citizens who take the trouble to vote in U.S. elections manage to turn up under their own steam. And the proportion of those who take part compared with the potentially eligible is distressingly low in the United States. Despite the novelty of Super Tuesday, it proved to be unexceptional in terms of grassroots excitement or participation.

Small differences at the precinct level, although virtually invisible to the naked eye, add up to aggregate trends which form the basis of election analysis. Jackson did well in the out-of-the-way areas of rural Georgia as well as urban centers such as Atlanta, but it was hard to tell in Dooly County on primary day, for example that anything special was going on. In Macon, Bibb County, a local referendum on increasing sales taxes stirred more notice among white voters than presidential rivalries. White Democrats in South Carolina, not used to turning out for arcane party caucuses, all but defaulted to the native son from Greenville. The engagement of rank-and-file African-Americans in the complicated process surprised even black elected officials, and though their numbers were modest, they loomed large in a select constituency.

Talking to voters as they went to vote in Georgia and South Carolina confirmed to this reporter that African-Americans were solid in their allegiance to Jackson, whereas white voters were relatively unenthusiastic about the Democratic alternatives. It was obvious that Reagan would have been the candidate of choice for a large proportion of white voters in both major parties. Even so, the turnout in the Republican primary (400,000 in Georgia, 195,000 in South Carolina) in both states was significantly large for the one-time "Solid South." Bush and Dole, the top G.O.P. vote-getters in Georgia, did nearly as well as Jackson and Gore's combined total.

Campaign workers testified that people seemed too busy these days to volunteer for the mundane tasks which are the stuff of local politics. Present-day restrictions on campaign contributions and the voracious cost of television exposure have all but wiped out bumper stickers, campaign buttons, billboards, and similar old-fashioned expressions of party activity. On the streets of Macon, Georgia, and Greenville, South Carolina, it was hard to tell an election was going on. Presumably, it was all being settled in front of the tube. With little funds for paid television, Jackson relied almost exclusively on word of mouth, especially from pulpits, and free exposure on the nightly television news. He did not seem to suffer from this deprivation among African-American voters, but whites less motivated to vote for Jackson saw and heard only the advertisements for white candidates.

The negatives expressed about Jackson at this early stage

by white voters and a handful of African-Americans seemed to be exacerbated largely by print media accounts of Jackson's past. His primary opponents steered away from direct attacks during televised debates or in their own negative advertising. Yet white voters in the precincts were never at a loss to berate Jackson for sins they were quick to cite. Some of their reservations were rooted in documented fact—his lack of experience in elected office; questions about his administrative capacities; his role in the aftermath of the assassination of Dr. Martin Luther King, Jr.; his enthusiastic support of the causes of trade unions, nuclear opponents, gays, and lesbians. Jackson's backers in the Super Tuesday states—even when they expressed doubts about one or more of these items—considered them irrelevant to the principal issue of the times, the crisis in national leadership and Jesse Jackson's unique abilities to lead and inspire. Jackson's critics were not all racists by any means. Some harbored sincere doubts about his obvious ego and flamboyant style; others were concerned about his positions on such knotty issues as the Middle East or abortion rights.

These are matters difficult to judge at the polling place where the decisions being expressed inside are locked in the emotions as well as the minds of individual voters.

Primary Day: Georgia

The state of Georgia was a key vantage point for observing the workings of Super Tuesday. It was one of those traditional members of the once Solid South that had strayed to the Republican column and Ronald Reagan in 1984. Walter Mondale had carried the Democratic primary that year although Jesse Jackson had garnered 20 percent of the vote (well below the percentage of voting-age African-Americans in the state). In 1986, Democrat Wyche Fowler had unseated a Republican incumbent in the U.S. Senate by dint of a white-black coalition at the polls. Home of both Senator Sam Nunn, a leader of Southern moderates, and approximately 450

African-American elected officials, Georgia could be regarded as a bellwether for the future of the Democratic Party in the South. It was regarded as a prime target for all the Democratic hopefuls in the 1988 presidential race.

Vienna, Dooly County

In Vienna, Georgia, 50 miles south of Macon on I-75, the rural and small-town South of yesteryear can still be seen. Vienna is in the 3rd Congressional District, where Sam Nunn and Jimmy Carter both reside. The district's population is 31 percent African-American, though that term is seldom heard around the Dooly County courthouse. In the town square is a statue of native son Walter George, once the patriarch of U.S. Senate conservatives, alongside the customary memorial to the soldiers of the Confederacy. The month before Super Tuesday, however, a black member of the city council had won a mayoral runoff against a white colleague in an election with a large turnout.

Inside Stan Gambrell's Shell station, just outside of town, only white faces were in evidence as men lingered over their morning coffee. Most, when queried, grumbled about the state of the Democratic Party. Allen Fulford, a retired state agricultural agent who happens to be a ringer for Jimmy Carter, grin and all, referred scathingly to "the peanut" over Plains way. He said he thought he might vote for Dole in that day's primary. John Joiner, a district committeeman for the Republicans, said he was pretty satisfied with the way things had been going under Reagan, but thought he might cast a vote for Jack Kemp rather than for Vice President Bush.

At the mention of Jesse Jackson, a couple of other farmers exchanged knowing grins. I mentioned that Jackson had seemed to make a hit with some white farmers while campaigning in Iowa. "I always thought pretty well of those farmers out there," said one, "until now." Laughter. Neither was much more enthusiastic about Gore. "Too much Washington in that feller," they agreed. But they weren't prepared to say how they might vote.

A well-dressed businessman was sitting by himself in a booth. He turned out to be the owner of the local radio station. He thought Dukakis had more on the ball than the rest of the field and noted that none of the candidates had bought any time on his station.

Half a mile down the road, inside Marise Country Kitchen, all the faces were black. Emerson Lundy, a Vietnam veteran and air-conditioning mechanic, said he was active in distributing posters for Jackson. "Reaganomics is killing us out here," he said. A middle-aged man sitting nearby nodded his agreement.

> Emerson Lundy, a Vietnam veteran and air-conditioning mechanic, said he was active in distributing posters for Jackson. "Reaganomics is killing us out here," he said.

The group proudly recalled that the new mayor of Vienna had been elected by 61 votes in the runoff in February. The churches played a big role, they said, in helping to register voters. The black candidate was a respected educator in the Dooly County school system; his white opponent, a longtime Vienna council member, did not have the greatest reputation for getting things done. The question on their minds was whether African-American voters could be turned out yet again, so soon, to vote for Jesse Jackson. They didn't expect many white votes in Dooly County for a black man running for president of the United States.

At the courthouse, voting was light at noon, 330 out of a voting list of 1,776 in Precinct 535. The total for the whole county at day's end was Jackson 858, Gore 510, Bush 191, Gephardt 131, Hart 125, Dole 107, Dukakis 72, Robertson 54, Kemp 29. That added up to roughly 43 percent for Jackson among the whole field, Republicans and Democrats, a percentage which was more than 10 points above the African-American proportion of the potential electorate. But overall turnout was down from 1984. Among Democrats, the figures were 50 percent for Jackson and 30 percent for Gore, better than Jackson's statewide showing. Gary Hart, ahead of both Senator Dole and Governor Dukakis in small-town Georgia? So much for straw polls at Gambrell's cafe.

Macon, Bibb County

In Macon, the Bibb County seat, local interest in the election was enhanced by a referendum on a city administration proposal to charge an extra penny on the local sales tax. The proceeds would be allocated to repair the county courthouse, expand the airport for the convenience of commercial travelers, build some new public library branches, and develop an industrial park in hopes of creating new jobs—in sum, a package seemingly appropriate to the New South. It was supported by most of the municipal establishment, but opposition from a grassroots organization had surfaced during the last week before Super Tuesday. At the local Jackson strategy meeting the night before there had been good-natured bantering over the issue between African-American elected officials present and rank-and-file Jackson supporters unenthusiastic over increased taxes. A consensus was reached that the official Jackson campaign in Macon should steer clear of the whole matter.

Bibb County is located in the 8th Congressional District, which weaves a narrow path through south-central Georgia. The area, 31 percent black, gave Wyche Fowler 57 percent of its vote in 1986.

The black-and-white Rainbow Coalition that gathered on the eve of the primary at Jackson headquarters in a Macon storefront included the son of a local white federal judge, who volunteered to drive folks to the polls on Super Tuesday. Three white students on spring break from a law school up North had been sent down from Atlanta to patrol polling places, making sure they were actually opened in rural areas and to advise precinct workers of their legal rights to assist voters asking for help with their ballots. Macon had just converted to a new electronic voting method in hopes of speeding the counting of votes. Old-timers, it was feared, might be intimidated by the unfamiliar process. Laurel Scott, a white former social worker, served as office manager, and her white husband, a candidate for delegate on the Jackson slate in the 8th district, checked out the availability of cars and drivers the next day. A black preacher from a nearby rural parish brought in a list of parishioners who might need transportation.

An African-American member of the city council passed the hat to finance sandwiches for election workers and, it was hoped, supplies for a victory party after the polls closed. Billy Young, the dynamic Jackson coordinator for South Georgia and a four-year veteran of the Rainbow Coalition, told the room how much it meant to him to see black and white, old and young, women and men, North and South, joined together, reaching out for new hope in America.

Laurel Scott recalled that in 1984, "whites did not feel welcome in the Jackson campaign in middle Georgia. This time it's different. I sat with Jesse at dinner when he came to Macon in November. He invited my husband to Raleigh for the announcement. The people who drop into headquarters are half white, half black. They leave a few dollars. Most don't tarry to pitch in these days. Everyone's busy with jobs and children. But we hope to keep this headquarters open after Super Tuesday to keep the coalition going so that it might take on a continuing role in politics in the 8th Congressional District." (On a trip through Macon in the spring of 1991, I found the old storefront closed.)

When primary day dawned, enthusiasm was at a high pitch at the Jackson campaign post, but the level of organization was modest. No one had prepared lists of voters which precinct workers could match against the names of those who came in to vote, standard practice in other parts of the country. Such lists enable volunteers to phone non-voters hour by hour and especially late in the day, in a last-ditch effort to persuade them to go to the polls and to offer them baby sitters or rides. In Macon on Super Tuesday, voters for the most part furnished their own momentum.

Whatever the stimulus, the flow of voters was steady throughout the day at both the John W. Burke School in a heavily black area on the east side of town and at the T.D. Tinsley School in a well-to-do residential section on the north side. It was a warm, muggy day, with the Japanese tulip trees already blossoming two weeks before the re-nowned Macon Cherry Blossom Festival. Get-out-the-vote public service spots were being broadcast intermittently on the local radio station.

At Burke, a 90-year-old African-American woman with failing sight was helped into the polls by one of the drivers from Jackson headquarters. He continued into the booth, helping her to fill in the small squares on the computer card. Many other older voters were accompanied by their chil-dren. Workers at the polls performed their duties in a crisp, businesslike fashion, with no hint of partisanship. There was no way of accurately estimating the turnout since campaign workers were forbidden to sit at the tables where the voting lists were being checked as voters filed in.

The occasional white voter I saw at Burke asked for a blue, Republican ballot. (There are no party registration rolls in Georgia.) One such couple, interviewed in the parking lot outside, conceded that they had never before voted Repub-lican. This time, they said, they had voted for Bush. Another white couple whom I had also observed picking up blue ballots slammed their car door when I approached them outside. "Lots of foolishness," the woman at the wheel muttered, "spending all that money," staking out her posi-tion on increasing the sales tax.

Up on the north side of town the voters were also racially mixed, but predominantly white and affluent. Many of the whites either refused to be interviewed or hurried away at the sight of a stranger. Republican ballots were definitely in higher demand here. Several women who said they were voting Democratic expressed admiration for Al Gore. "He's such a gentleman," said one. Younger whites here tended to ask for Republican ballots, as did one or two well dressed African-Americans. "I've been doing okay," said one of the latter when asked his opinion about the Reagan administration. "Don't see any reason for a change now."

The final turnout at the Tinsley School precinct was 55.5 percent, 727 voters out of an eligible 1,309. Just over half (57.6 percent) had chosen to vote Republican, although Gore finished with more votes than Bush, the G.O.P. leader. At the Burke School, Jesse Jackson won hands down, beating Gore and Dukakis by better than 20 to one. Turnout (42 percent) was markedly lower than on the more affluent north side, although nine out of 10 voted Democratic. The actual tally in the two Macon precincts illustrated the difference between these Georgia constituencies, one overwhelmingly black and characterized by modest incomes, the other principally white and middle-class.

At the Burke School, Godfrey Precinct 1, the total was Jackson 539, Gore 25, Dukakis 23, Robertson 17, Bush 10, Dole eight, Gephardt four, Hart three, Kemp two, Babbitt one, DuPont one. Over at the Tinsley School, Vineville Precinct 8: Gore 185, Bush 149, Jackson 113, Dole 93, Dukakis 70, Robertson 53, Gephardt 21, Hart 10, Simon nine, Kemp seven, Babbitt one, Haig one.

The spread of these choices illustrates the rich diversity of individual Americans when it comes to expressing their voting preferences. Come hell or high water, there are always those prepared to stick with their favorites against the popular tide. But it also illustrates the importance of demographics in analyzing election statistics. At Godfrey Precinct 1, Jackson polled 82 percent of the overall total on Super Tuesday. At Vineville Precinct 8, in the same town, his portion of the total came to 15.5 percent. At the Godfrey precinct the proposed sales tax was voted down, 416 to 184.

At the Vineville precinct the sales-tax referendum split straight down the middle, 351 in favor, 351 opposed.

The overall turnout in Macon-Bibb County on Super Tuesday came to a record 51 percent of the county's 68,234 registered voters. Nearly one-third of those votes were cast for Republican candidates, a strong GOP showing for that part of Georgia. Jackson polled 11,248 votes, 48 percent of the Democratic tally. Gore, who had been endorsed by the local paper, finished second with 7,091. The results in Bibb County exceeded Jackson's margin in the state as a whole, where he polled 39.7 percent (36 delegates) against 32.4 percent (31 delegates) for Gore and 15.6 percent (10 delegates) for Dukakis.

General turnout in the Georgia primary was higher than in any other Deep South state, but in Macon more black voters stayed home than went to the polls.

By the time of the Democratic national convention in July, the Gore delegates had switched to Dukakis. George Bush dominated the Republican side in Macon-Bibb County with 45.7 percent, well ahead of Dole and Robertson.

The proposed sales tax went down, 19,603 to 14,198, a result which, the Macon *Telegraph and News* reported, astonished city and county elected officials. "It's the people out there who speak," said Bibb Commission Chairman Emory Green. "We did something bad wrong. I thought it was a good idea, but it's the people out there who speak. I listen and take the lesson."

General turnout in Georgia, according to the Southern Legislative Conference, was higher (40 percent) than in any other Deep South state. But the turnout figures in Macon's black precincts indicated that more black voters stayed home than went to the polls, even when they had a chance to vote for a charismatic African-American presidential candidate. Among the priorities of survival, choosing among politicians is not very high to the disadvantaged poor.

Exit polls by CBS and ABC indicated that Jackson received 93 to 94 percent of the black vote in the state, as against 6 to 7 percent of the white vote. The latter was double Jackson's showing in 1984, but came nowhere near the figures which had elected Wyche Fowler in 1986. Neither the African-American turnout nor Jackson's percentage was as exceptional as one might have deduced from Northern press accounts of Jackson's Super Tuesday victories. This harsh fact about the primary political process in the year of Jesse Jackson's breakthrough candidacy calls for fuller evaluation as Democrats debate the political future of their party. The disconnection of so many Americans seems greatest among traditional Democrats—ethnic minorities, the less educated, the young, and the less well-to-do.

Caucus Day: South Carolina

South Carolina had refused to go along with 14 other Southern and border states in scheduling a presidential primary on a common date in March 1988. The two parties, however, took different approaches to the process.

The Republicans agreed to hold a primary, but, in a shrewd stroke, scheduled it for March 5, the Saturday before Super Tuesday. Any voter could participate by signing a pledge not to take part in a subsequent Democratic contest. Though difficult to enforce, the provision had a preemptive psychological effect, predisposing voters to think of themselves as Republicans before they could be recruited by Democratic rivals. It also assured the Palmetto State the national spotlight as the media moved South after Iowa and New Hampshire. The interest was intensified when Pat Robertson, who had unexpectedly finished ahead of Vice President Bush in Iowa, predicted he would beat Bush again when they reached the church-going precincts of South Carolina. Bush, Robertson, Dole, and Kemp all toured the state, followed by the television networks, photographers, and political correspondents

71

from the major national and regional newspapers.

Republican Governor Carroll Campbell, Jr., an early Bush backer, demonstrated the ability of his organization to play political hardball. Voters in rural areas, where Robertson might be expected to do well, found many of their regular polling places closed on primary day and had to drive miles to unfamiliar locations in order to cast a ballot. In contrast, all the precincts in the metropolitan areas of Columbia, Greenville, and Spartanburg were fully manned. A state-of-the-art press center was set up on the state fairgrounds in Columbia for television cameras, photographers, and word processors to spread the word that George Bush had swept the Republican South Carolina primary (better than two-to-one over both Dole and Robertson) in a record-breaking (195,292) turnout. South Carolina proved to be the spring-board for a similar sweep of all the Republican Super Tuesday primaries, all but clinching the nomination for George Bush and foreshadowing his electoral sweep of the South in November. (Lee Atwater, a native son, went on to become Republican national chairman at the request of the new President, cementing South Carolina's new stature in the party.)

On the other hand, the Democratic chairman in South Carolina, Don Fowler, never concealed his distaste for the whole Super Tuesday idea. Instead of a primary, Democrats chose to stay with the traditional caucus system. Caucus meetings through the years had customarily been attended by a handful of party insiders who usually voted to stay uncommitted until the national convention, where the South Carolina delegation had frequently moved in a bloc. In the days of the old politics and a one-party South, such tactics were commonplace. But nowadays nominations were usually locked up before the convention even opened. And to compound the problem, South Carolina Democrats chose to hold their caucuses on March 12, the Saturday after Super Tuesday. By this time, most of the candidates and the national media had moved on to Illinois for the next phase of the campaign in the Midwest.

Thus the window of opportunity opened for Jesse Jackson, born and raised in Greenville, South Carolina, to return to his native state as a candidate for the Democratic nomination for president of the United States. Greenville is in the 4th Congressional District, won narrowly by a Democrat in 1986, although the Republican candidate carried Greenville County. Part of South Carolina's industrialized upcountry, the city is typical of metropolitan areas throughout the New South. It voted 70 percent for Ronald Reagan and is the home of Governor Campbell. The African-American population is 17 percent, compared with a statewide average of 27 percent. Greenville today is a far cry from the place where Jesse Jackson grew up in poverty, raised in a public housing project by a teen-aged mother. Although many African-Americans there persist in a state of poverty, a substantial middle class populates business, education, and the professions. Affluent or poor, blacks in Greenville are united by a growing self-consciousness of their power in state political affairs.

On caucus day there was not much visible political activity except for a few posters supporting Jackson, Gephardt, and Dukakis. After winning Iowa, Gephardt had been belatedly endorsed by former governors Dick Riley and Bob McNair and by three out of the four Democrats in the state's congressional delegation. He had made a brief swing through the state, but was concentrating most of his efforts in a last-ditch stand in Michigan after having averaged only 13.1 percent in the Super Tuesday states, a figure inflated by the 57.8 percentage tallied in his home state of Missouri. Senator Gore's campaign had gone into abeyance when South Carolina proved to be one of the few states in the Deep South where he was not endorsed by the local organization, and was now twisting slowly in the wind.

Jackson's field organization in North Carolina, where he had finished behind Gore by only a slim margin, came across the border to lend a hand. They were instructed, however, to stay out of Greenville where "Jesse likes to do things his own way." Jackson, locked in a struggle with Senator Paul Simon and Governor Michael Dukakis for Illinois' 200 delegates, flew back to Greenville on caucus day.

Greenville, Precinct 12

At four o'clock on the afternoon of Saturday, March 12, Greenville's Precinct 12 caucus site was scheduled to open along with 1,779 other Democratic caucuses around the state. No one was there. The voting place was a recreation building in Cleveland Park, a former skating rink set among some tennis courts, and a few African-American kids were playing pick-up basketball.

The day was warm and muggy, punctuated by occasional showers. The finals of the Atlantic Coast Conference basketball tournament between arch rivals Duke and North Carolina were on television and radio. In these parts that constituted a potent rival attraction to politics. At the appointed hour, two men dressed in coveralls strolled up to the front door. The door was locked. "Ain't they voting here today?" asked one. I said they were. They decided to wait.

Perhaps a half-dozen had gathered by the time a park attendant arrived 15 minutes later to open a side door. The attendant led them into a dark, cavernous gymnasium with a set of bleachers behind the basket at one end. The rest of the floor was bare. As they took their places, a harried-looking, smartly dressed woman arrived with two helpers carrying a folding table which they set up along the foul line. She turned out to be Mrs. Theo Walker Mitchell, Precinct 12 president and the wife of State Senator Mitchell, who was not far behind. Senator Mitchell, a handsome, courtly man, well tailored and wearing a golden palmetto tree pin on his coat, welcomed the first arrivals with a friendly greeting and handshake. In a phone conversation earlier in the day he had predicted that about a dozen or 13 might show up at the late afternoon caucus. He said he intended to run as a Jackson delegate.

Next to arrive was a party of five, two men and three women, white and elderly. They took their place on the bleachers near the door. If Senator Mitchell's turnout prediction proved to be correct, it looked to be an interesting afternoon for his candidacy. Suddenly, with the swiftness of an ice-jam breaking up, a steady stream of persons began filing in to take their place on the bleachers—young and old, poor and comfortably off, neighborly women and men engaged in good-natured needling. All were black, and all seemed serious and purposeful.

Shortly after four-thirty the attendance was close to 50, about a dozen of them white. One of the latter took a place at the official table, dandling in her lap a red-headed girl dressed in a pinafore and white stockings. "I think I'm vice chairman of the precinct," she announced, somewhat tentatively. Mrs. Mitchell smiled a confirmation. By four forty-five the bleachers were nearly full.

Chatting amiably, Senator Mitchell told me he and Jesse Jackson had played football together at Sterling High in the fifties. "Jesse was always a very innovative quarterback," he recalled. "The coach would send in a play, but Jesse would call one of his own," he laughed.

It was time to conduct business. Mrs. Mitchell read the party orders, including instructions that party officers as well as delegates should include women, minorities, and all economic groups. The hat was then passed to cover the cost of holding the caucus. She then asked all present to come forward and sign a pledge that they had not participated this year in the nominating process of another political party. As far as one could see there were no voting lists available (as had been evident at Republican polling places a week earlier) to verify the eligibility of those present. The line to sign the pledge was time-consuming, and the bleachers were getting restless.

But first, precinct officers needed to be elected for the coming year. Vernon Kennedy, a retired federal marshal wearing a Jackson button and an Omega Psi Phi fraternity hat, was elected president without opposition. It was explained that under the rules, the first vice president had to be white and second vice president had to be under 30. A slate was duly nominated and elected with the husband of the incumbent vice president succeeding her in office. By now it was well after five. A motion was made and passed unanimously that henceforth Democratic presidential caucuses in South Carolina should be replaced by a primary. A voice from the bleachers asked, "Will the new officers stand up so we can see who they are?" It was done. An hour had gone by and the time had come for the main business.

The new precinct president issued instructions: all those who wanted to send delegates to the state convention who would support Jesse Jackson for president should remain in the bleachers. Supporters for Senator Gore and Governor Dukakis should gather at each end of the sideline on the left. Supporters for Richard Gephardt, Paul Simon, and those preferring the South Carolina delegation to remain uncommitted should gather in groups along the right sideline. (Surprisingly, as the votes were being counted a tally clerk asked my wife and me, standing ambiguously on the sidelines, for whom we wanted to vote. We hastily informed him that we were outside observers.)

A group of eight, including the five early arrivals plus three other whites, took their place in the area reserved for Gore. Nobody gathered for either Dukakis or Simon. Four––three whites and a retired African-American schoolteacher—marched from the bleachers to the Gephardt area to the right. The teacher said Governor Riley had always been a friend of education, "and if he thinks Gephardt would be the best candidate, that's good enough for me." Three whites—two young women who said they were paralegals and a white lawyer who had been elected a precinct officer—assembled as uncommitted. The rest, 84 out of 99 present, remained in the bleachers to be counted for Jesse Jackson. Two of those faces were white, a teacher and a student from North Greenville College.

Under the rules, the precinct was entitled to 26 delegates to the county convention, distributed according to the size of each group. At the county level, the process would be repeated and delegates sent to the state convention. At a ratio of 84 out of 99, Jackson's share added up to 22 delegates, an overwhelming majority.

The last order of business was for each group to pick the delegates to the county convention. (Senator Mitchell was among those chosen. Later, he was bumped off the Jackson delegation to Atlanta, he said, when he failed to vote for the candidate for state Democratic chairman endorsed by Jackson backers.)

Shortly after 6:00 p.m. the totals were dispatched to Wade Hampton High School out past Bob Jones University, to be tallied together with the other precincts in Greenville County. There, returns from the county precincts were chalked up on a blackboard while party workers ate barbecue, beans, cole-slaw, chips, and Pepsi-Cola at six bucks a head. There were few black faces on the chow line, however. They were already on the way to Greenville Tech for a scheduled victory rally for the homecoming hero.

The delegate total for Greenville County was: Jackson 1,036, Gore 410, Dukakis 219, uncommitted 138, Gephardt 50, Simon nine. That came to 56 percent for Jackson in a jurisdiction where few African-Americans could vote when he was growing up there. Statewide, the same averages were holding: the final count was Jackson 54.8 percent, Gore 16.8, uncommitted 19.9, Dukakis 6.3, Gephardt 1.8, and Simon 0.4. (When state delegates were chosen Jackson was awarded 23 out of 44. One of the superdelegates, Senator Ernest F. Hollings, declared for Jackson in June, but most of the others declared themselves uncommitted and ended up voting for Dukakis.) Total participation in the Democratic caucuses in South Carolina came to 45,000, less than a fourth the number who voted in the Republican primaries. The ratio was not that much different in November.

Homecoming

Oblivious to the rain and occasional lightning outside, a jubilant crowd began early to fill up the library auditorium at Greenville Technical College. It was a rainbow audience beneath the huge "Welcome Home Jesse" banner, listening to a five-piece band (saxophones, electric organ, guitar, and drums) playing "I Just Called to Say I Love You." Vernon Kennedy, the new president of Precinct 12, now dressed to the nines, was one of the ushers. "Jesse Jackson '88" signs and a row of American flags decorated a stage festooned with red, white, and blue balloons. The press section was already crowded with television cameras in anticipation of the candidate's arrival.

"I was raised in public housing over there in Fieldcrest Village," Jackson told a crowd in his hometown of Greenville, South Carolina.

Outside, television satellite uplink vans and Secret Service men in earplugs were at the ready when a bus carrying the national Jackson press wheeled up to the entrance. As usual, they had become separated from the candidate.

Back inside, a choir director continues to warm up the crowd: "Jesse is the best—the best is Jesse. We're gonna make him Pres-i-dent: When? 1988!" The band strikes up "My County 'Tis of Thee" and Jackson sweeps into the hall through a rear door to a rising chorus of cheers and applause. With him is his mother, Helen Jackson, his grandmother, Matilda, his elementary school teacher, his high school football coach, plus a coterie of local politicians and a lanky white man wearing a large broad-rimmed hat with a rainbow symbol. He turns out to be John Jay Hooker, one-time Kennedy field supervisor and candidate for governor in Tennessee. He seems to have a penchant for crowding into photo opportunities and no one is sure of his precise role within the

78

Jackson entourage.

After touching down in Greenville shortly after six, Jackson had gone to the Phyllis Wheatley Center to shake hands with members of the Democratic caucus just breaking up. The local press, the *Greenville News and Piedmont*, would report the next day:

"Jackson said his message crossed racial lines and that his concerns for farmers, education and issues involving welfare families were concerns for all. Jackson then abruptly announced that he was going to his old Fieldcrest Village apartment and proceeded on foot to the nearby housing complex with his mother and grandmother.

"At the steps of his old apartment residence, now that of Barbara Smith and her family, Jackson lamented the economic plight of families who live in subsidized housing and said he only overcame his own environment because of a strong family."

The trip to Fieldcrest Village, Jesse explains to the crowd which has waited two hours at Greenville Tech, has delayed his arrival. "I just had to stop off for some of my mama's cornbread and collard greens." He is forgiven in an instant.

"I was raised in public housing over there in Fieldcrest Village," he goes on, sweeping his arm in the direction from which he has come. "Now, I don't mind moving into public housing at sixteen hundred Pennsylvania Avenue. The taxpayers pay for both. Just because you were born in the slum, there needn't be a slum in you.

"Tonight I was determined to share this moment with you, this wonderful moment in our campaign of hope. I don't know what the future holds, but I know who holds the future. We, the people, can win." The audience cheers its response. "We, the people, can win. We, the people, can win." Jesse, beaming, hugs his schoolteacher, then his mother, then his grandmother. He waves his arms to the rocking crowd and shouts over the din, "Come to the inauguration!"

7

Who Won?

When the votes were counted on Super Tuesday, Jesse Jackson had polled better than 2.5 million, won the most delegates (330), carried five states (Virginia, Mississippi, Alabama, Georgia, Louisiana), which would become six after the caucuses in South Carolina, and lost by an eyelash in a seventh (North Carolina). Perhaps most important of all, Jackson was now accepted by the mass media and the Democratic Party establishment as a serious player in the presidential nominating process.

At the same time, two of Jackson's opponents could also claim victories of their own. Senator Al Gore had won 318 delegates, carried five states (Tennessee, Kentucky, Oklahoma, Arkansas, North Carolina) and led Jackson by the narrowest of margins in the overall vote percentage (27.6 percent to 27.3 percent). Now established as a vote-getter in the white South, Gore's next challenge would be to demonstrate his pulling power outside his native region. Governor Michael Dukakis not only finished first in two mega-state contests (Florida, Texas) plus one border state (Maryland), but won delegates in the metropolitan suburbs of North Carolina, Georgia, and several other states. The number of delegates he won on Super Tuesday (259) moved him toward the top of the pack as the primary schedule headed

North, favorable turf for him to solidify a claim to be the front-runner.

Four out of 10 white voters in the South chose to participate in the Republican primary, even though George Bush was heavily favored after his smashing victory in South Carolina; he won every Super Tuesday state. Republicans polled over five million votes (98 percent white), affirming the party's presence in the once Democratic South.

None of this, of course, matched the expectations of the originators of the Super Tuesday experiment. Congressman Richard Gephardt ran poorly outside of his home base in Missouri. Virginia, where former governor Charles Robb had been one of the earliest sponsors, provided Jackson with his highest primary percentage (45 percent), and delivered 15 delegates to Dukakis, whose statewide showing (21.8 percent) approximated Gore's (22.5 percent). Although Gore won in North Carolina, there was a substantially lower turnout of Democratic voters than four years earlier, contrary to the hopes that Super Tuesday would swell voter participation. Democratic turnout was also down in Georgia and Alabama. Republicans, on the other hand, turned out in record numbers in Florida, Georgia, South Carolina, Texas, and Virginia.

The Jackson success was less an outpouring of newly motivated African-American voters than the product of these skewed turns in the electorate. Jackson's top showing in Virginia was attained in a state where overall turnout was the lowest of all 14 primary states (23 percent) and where a substantial number of white voters (200,000) opted for the Republican ballot.

In North Carolina, Jackson's 1988 raw vote was actually smaller than in 1984 (224,177 versus 243,945) although Mondale and Hart had scored more heavily in African-American precincts than did Gore and Dukakis. Turnout was down generally in the Tarheel State because, unlike in 1984, there was no heated primary for statewide offices. North Carolina is a rare state where voting registration is still recorded by race. Even if every vote Jackson received had been cast by an African-American, which was not the case, it would still mean that only about 36 percent of the 589,203 potential registered black voters had turned out to support his candidacy—not an overwhelming turnout in the state where Jackson had announced his candidacy and where organizational efforts had started early.

Registration of new voters throughout the South in 1988 lacked funding and organization. Jackson's presidential campaign in 1984 was perceived as a symbolic effort in which voting registration was a priority as part of a general strategy to enhance the local political power of African-Americans. The registration drive continued for the crucial 1986 off-year elections. In the 1988 Jackson effort, the media pressures and nationwide drive for delegates diverted time, energy, and money from registration endeavors. Stories in the national press about Super Tuesday suggesting that the Jackson phenomenon was the result of an outpouring of new armies of African-American voters were to find scant documentation in registration and turnout figures.

That is not to say that Jackson's Super Tuesday showing was not marked by extraordinary enthusiasm among his followers. Jackson's percentages in Super Tuesday states were substantially higher than the proportion of voting age African-Americans in each constituency. That could not have been accomplished without lots of hard work and inspiration at the grassroots.

There is a significant correlation, however, between the level of the Jackson vote in each state and the percentage of blacks in the voting-age population, as the figures in the following table illustrate.

The ratio between the percentages of blacks in the voting-age population and the percentages tallied by Jackson on Super Tuesday varied from state to state, although he generally polled a higher percentage than the black share of the electorate. Factors such as turnout, the campaign priorities of rival candidates, the number of whites who chose to vote in

Super Tuesday Votes

	Black % of Voting-Age Population	Jackson	Gore	Dukakis	Gephardt
South Carolina*	27%	54.8%	16.8%	6.3%	1.8%
Virginia	18	45.1	22.3	22.0	4.4
Mississippi	31	44.4	33.3	8.3	5.4
Alabama	23	43.6	37.4	7.7	7.4
Georgia	24	39.8	32.4	15.6	6.7
Louisiana	28	35.5	28.0	15.3	10.6
North Carolina	20	33.0	34.7	20.3	5.5
Maryland	24	28.7	8.7	45.6	7.9
Texas	11	24.5	20.2	32.8	13.6
Tennessee	15	20.7	72.3	3.4	1.5
Missouri	10	20.2	2.8	11.6	57.8
Florida	12	20.0	12.7	40.9	14.4
Arkansas	14	17.1	37.3	18.9	12.0
Kentucky	7	15.6	45.8	18.6	9.1
Oklahoma	6	13.3	41.4	16.9	21.1
Total		27.3	27.6	23.5	13.1
No. of Delegates		330	318	259	94

* South Carolina caucuses held March 12.
Source: Southern Legislative Conference, from certified returns.

the Republican Party, and different levels of local organization each contributed to the result. But these percentages tell only part of the story.

In Georgia, for example, Jackson increased his 1984 primary total by 104,000 votes, but the number participating in the Democratic primary decreased by 62,000. Over 400,000 (39 percent of those voting) selected the Republican ballot. So Jackson won a larger slice of a smaller pie as Georgia whites defected to the GOP column.

In North Carolina, Jackson actually polled *fewer* votes than he had in 1984, but the number voting in the Democratic primary fell by a whopping 281,000 as 274,000 voted in the

Republican presidential contest (in 1984, there had been no GOP primary since Reagan was running for re-election).

Thus, with a contest for an open nomination to the White House, the Republican Party found Super Tuesday a valuable vehicle for recruiting potential voters in November. Over a million voted in the Republican primary in Florida and 900,000 in Texas. In a three-way fight on the Democratic side, two whites versus an African-American, Jackson's percentages increased over what they had been four years before in five of the seven states which held Democratic presidential primaries in both years, but he did best where Democratic turnout fell generally.

Special circumstances affected the comparisons in the two states where Jackson's percentages actually fell: There had been a white boycott of the 1984 Louisiana primary, and favorite son Al Gore was running in Tennessee in 1988. Florida and Maryland were special targets of the Dukakis campaign, and he carried both by wide margins in heavier 1988 turnouts of Democrats. Jackson improved his showing substantially in both states, but 44 percent and 38 percent (respectively) of the voters went Republican, double the pro-

Democratic Primary Vote: 1984 and 1988

	Jackson Percentage		Democratic Turnout	
	1984	1988	1984	1988
Alabama	19.6	43.6	428,283	405,642
Georgia	21.0	39.8	684,541	622,752
Louisiana	42.9	35.5	318,810	624,450
North Carolina	25.4	33.0	960,857	679,958
Maryland	26.0	28.7	506,166	531,335
Tennessee	25.0	20.7	322,033	576,014
Florida	12.2	20.0	1,182,190	1,273,298
Total			4,402,880	4,713,749

Source: Southern Legislative Conference.

portion of four years earlier.

According to exit polls conducted in the Super Tuesday states by NBC, ABC, and CBS, approximately 95 percent of African-Americans who voted cast their ballots for Jackson, although he received less than 90 percent in Texas, Florida, and Maryland, where Dukakis ran best. (Among Latinos, Jackson and Dukakis split the vote almost evenly, although Dukakis won by better than two-to-one in Florida and Texas, where he concentrated his Super Tuesday efforts.)

Jackson exceeded his average in places with the highest concentration of African-Americans. Jackson's highest percentages were in Southern congressional districts containing the largest cities: 75 percent in Georgia's 5th Congressional District (Atlanta); 72 percent in Tennessee's 9th Congressional District (Memphis); 65 percent in Maryland's 7th Congressional District (Baltimore); 63 percent in Alabama's 6th Congressional District (Birmingham); and 60 percent in Virginia's 3rd Congressional District (Richmond).

Jackson called for a New South in which there would be economic as well as racial equality. "We must stop jobs from flowing out of the country; 1.6 million Southerners were displaced from their jobs between 1974 and 1985," he said. "One in seven Southern farmers lost their livelihood between 1984 and 1986. . . . Ensuring a fair price, providing debt relief and returning lost land to . . . minority farmers are the solution."

He went on: "We must provide health care to all Americans, regardless of their pocketbook or where they live. Thirteen million Southerners have no health insurance and rural hospitals are dying . . . . We must protect our environment—three Southern states account for more than half the hazardous-waste dump capacity in the country." And: "We must provide Head Start and day care on the front side of life, not jail care and welfare on the back side."

The dramatic response to Jackson by poor African-Americans living in the big-city slums of Atlanta, Memphis, and Baltimore was even exceeded in poor rural counties such as

Greene County, Alabama (86 percent) and Hancock County, Georgia (80 percent). Asked by ABC News to describe the personal characteristic that most influenced their choice, 51 percent of Jackson voters on Super Tuesday picked "understands people like me," and four in 10 cited "strong leader" who would "bring changes." One in three said they were voting for the first time.

Media fascination with the Super Tuesday horse race and delegate count tended to obscure the fact that relatively few Southerners (33.6 percent of those registered to vote, which in turn is only a fraction of the voting-age population) opted to take part in the presidential primary process. Jackson's excellent showing, so valuable to his political credibility in the party and the press, did not involve a huge outpouring of voters, a fact largely overlooked at the time by the media.

In spite of massive publicity, a national spotlight, and intensive campaigning across the South, in spite of the charismatic character of the African-American standard-bearer, in spite of the motivation furnished by racial pride in Jackson's position as a top contender for the presidency, a majority of the African-American population simply did not come out to vote. The overall turnout for Super Tuesday came to 34 percent, not bad in comparison to the number of Americans who participate in presidential primaries in the rest of the nation. Black turnout on average was somewhat higher. But the nature of the electoral process has become increasingly uninviting to masses of Americans as the percentages of those who participate in the presidential general elections continue to drop. In such an environment, it is perhaps too much to expect the poorest minorities to vote in spectacular numbers.

Assessing the gains registered by Jackson in 1988 as against 1984 is complicated by the fact that Super Tuesday included states which had not held primaries in '84. And Walter Mondale, endorsed by black leaders in Alabama and Georgia, had siphoned off African-American votes which went better than 90 percent for Jackson this time. In the seven

Southern states which held primaries in both presidential years, the Jackson vote increased by 49 percent. But that comes to fewer than half-a-million votes. And a quarter-million of those were African-Americans who were Mondale or Hart voters in '84. Jackson increased his white share by a few percentage points, although still polling fewer than 10 percent. Thus Jackson's net gain among blacks—new voters minus dropouts—in these states probably amounted to less than 20 percent.

Jackson Vote in Southern Primaries

	1984	1988
Alabama	84,000	178,000
Georgia	144,000	248,000
Louisiana	137,000	220,000
Maryland	132,000	154,000
Tennessee	81,000	119,000
Florida	114,000	256,000
Total	966,000	1,399,000
Total Jackson gain, 1984 to 1988:		433,000

The originators of Super Tuesday had complained about the small number of voters in atypical states such as Iowa and New Hampshire having a disproportionate effect on presidential politics. Yet this experiment with a regional primary did not attract a substantially increased proportion of voters.

Breaking Down the Numbers

Virginia turned in the lowest overall turnout (23 percent) of all the Super Tuesday primary states and, at the same time, it was where Jackson won 38 delegates and scored his highest proportion of the Democratic vote (45.1 percent). It was the first presidential primary ever in the state (on the

Republican side there was a non-binding "beauty contest" with the delegates to be chosen later). Computations by Professor Larry Sabato of the University of Virginia estimate that the turnout in black precincts was 39.1 percent. Portsmouth, where the legendary Bishop L. E. Willis presides, cast 55.2 percent of its registered votes and 96.8 percent of that went to Jackson. The story was the same in other African-American strongholds: Norfolk, 41.5 percent turnout, 95 percent Jackson; Richmond, 32.9 percent turnout, 91.9 percent Jackson. He also scored heavily in rural Surrey County, with 84 percent. The top African-American elected official in Virginia, Lieutenant Governor L. Douglas Wilder, who was planning his run for governor in 1989, did not endorse Jackson and remained aloof from the election. In the end, Jackson did handsomely among the black constituency and Wilder maintained a non-threatening image among whites.

The Republican primary attracted 234,745 voters compared to 366,599 in the Democratic contest, one of the highest such ratios in the South. Elsewhere on Super Tuesday, 45 percent of those who voted for Gore described themselves as Republican. Former Democratic governor Charles Robb and Attorney General Mary Sue Terry both endorsed Gore. But Gore ended up with less than half Jackson's total, most of it polled in the west country adjacent to Tennessee where he won all his 22 delegates. Michael Dukakis won his 15 delegates from the Northern Virginia suburbs across the Potomac from the District of Columbia and ran nearly even with Gore in statewide percentages. Fairfax County in Northern Virginia went 34 percent for Dukakis and 18 percent for Jackson; Jackson led Dukakis, 44 percent to 29 percent, in Charlottesville, site of the University of Virginia. One in five of those white voters who described themselves as "liberal" voted for Jackson although double that proportion voted for Dukakis.

Nearly 80 percent of those Virginians who voted for Jackson, interviewed by CBS as they left the polls, said they had made up their mind to do so before 1988 had even begun. Jackson topped all the others in voter perceptions of a "strong leader," but rated lowest on "experience." Among voters with incomes below $12,500 a year, voters preferred Jackson to Dukakis by nearly four-to-one. A clear majority of Jackson voters picked poverty and unemployment as the issues that mattered most to them. On national defense, Gore was the clear favorite in the field. Dukakis did best on Nicaragua, but fewer than 10 percent thought that issue "mattered." One-third said they were concerned about the federal deficit, but did not differentiate very much on their estimates of each candidate's ability to do something about it.

Florida (42 percent), second only to Arkansas (47 percent) in Super Tuesday turnout, is perhaps the least "Southern" of the 14 states that participated in the regional primary experiment. Voting-age blacks comprise only 11 percent of the Florida electorate. Dukakis, in carrying the state, scored heavily in network exit polls among Catholic, Jewish, and Latino voters, although a substantial number of the latter voted in the Republican primary. The party split in Florida was 40 percent Republican versus 60 percent Democratic, an even higher ratio than in Virginia, and Gore won only six Democratic delegates against 90 for Dukakis and 33 for Jackson in these circumstances.

Forty-two percent of Florida's population is over 60 and Dukakis won a clear majority of this key age group, according to exit polls. Jackson won only one percent from Jewish voters compared to Dukakis's 78 percent. Dukakis won 59 percent of white Catholics as well as 39 percent of white Protestants. Jackson supporters, however, showed the highest intensity in supporting their candidate; 38 percent of Dukakis voters, on the other hand, said they were backing him because they disliked the alternatives.

The Rainbow Coalition

Gerald Austin, Jackson's campaign manager, projected that the best-case scenario for his candidate on Super Tuesday would involve (1) an unprecedented turnout of black voters, (2) double-digit percentages of white voters responding to the Rainbow Coalition, and (3) substantial defections of conservative white Democrats choosing to vote for Pat Robertson in the Republican primary. None of these possibilities actually occurred. Jackson's showing, therefore, is all the more remarkable.

As we have seen, African-Americans rallied to the Jackson candidacy, but their turnout was down in North Carolina compared to 1984 and there were no dramatic increases in voter registration. According to CBS exit polls, those who said they were voting for the first time split 31 percent for Jackson, 26 percent for Dukakis, 23 percent for Gore, and 13 percent for Gephardt, a substantial but not overwhelming Jackson advantage. White candidates campaigned only nominally among African-Americans, but polled 10 percent or better of African-American votes in Florida, Maryland, Kentucky, Missouri, and Oklahoma.

Senator Albert Gore scored heavily among white rural and religious voters, carrying such traditionally conservative counties as Lamar, Alabama (48 percent); George, Mississippi (48 percent); and Echols, Georgia (42 percent). The CBS polls showed that Gore was supported by 42 percent of whites identifying themselves as "conservative," 42 percent of white fundamentalist or evangelical Christians, 37 percent of whites under 30 (versus nine percent for Jackson) and 36 percent of those who had voted for Reagan in 1984.

Jackson's overall vote among women in the Super Tuesday states ran about five points ahead of those cast by males, but that margin was mostly among black, not white, women. The gender gap among whites was working mainly for Dukakis. Looked at another way, Gore was the candidate of choice among white males. Jackson won support among some women for his stands on education, abortion, and disarmament, but that aspect of the Rainbow Coalition approach did not achieve a major breakthrough.

The strength shown by Dukakis among Latino voters diluted another hoped-for rainbow constituency. Polls have larger margins of error among relatively small ethnic segments, but CBS exit polls reported that Jackson received the backing of 21 percent of Mexican-Americans in Texas, while 52 percent went for Dukakis. ABC put the Dukakis advantage over Jackson at 60-20, NBC at 47-28. Dukakis campaigned in Spanish and mounted an extensive direct-mail effort. He carried Starr County on the Rio Grande by a wide margin and ran strongly across South Texas. Three percent of the ballots in the Republican primary were cast by Latinos.

Tuscarora Indians in North Carolina's Robeson County, however, voted for Jackson by larger numbers in 1988 than in 1984, bucking the statewide turnout trend. Jackson's vote in that county went from 5,928 to 8,618, an outcome that was satisfying symbolically but did not make much of a dent in Gore's plurality elsewhere.

Bruce Lightner, the North Carolina Jackson coordinator, cited one example of Jesse's effort in that state to reach out for white voters. Fishermen along the state's eastern coast were in a jam because a red tide of algae had killed off the fish. "Jesse took a boat out of Wilmington and held a press conference on the problem out at sea. Candidates foam at the mouth for free media like Jesse drew on that. It symbolized Jesse's interest in working men's problems, whatever their race. Two days after Jesse's trip we got a call from a food bank saying they would send food, four tons of it, to the fishermen if we could supply the transportation. We asked the truckers to carry it, and they agreed. We didn't hold a press conference about that. But we carried Pender and Brunswick counties this time, where we ran third in '84—and lost New Hanover by only four votes, where we also ran third four years ago.

"After New Hampshire, Austin sent in a group of six young white people who had been working up there. Three went on to work in Florida. They came with a fax machine, something I didn't have. I called them 'the Hampshires.' They worked hard. It was good to see such commitment to Jesse from white folk.... They got along fine with everyone. I'd like to show you a letter Steve Canzian, a kid from California who had been living in New Hampshire and working for Gary Hart, wrote me: 'Thank you for letting us all get involved without politics and turf battles. Thank you for trusting us'.... I'm not sure how all the votes went, but you could see rainbow walk in the door of our Raleigh headquarters. A white maid at one of the local headquarters, a white construction worker, they came to volunteer."

Jackson polled 32 percent of the vote in Orange County, home of the University of North Carolina, where African-Americans made up only 14 percent of the registered Democrats. Orange is considered the state's most liberal county. But it was Dukakis who carried Chapel Hill.

Appealing to a white constituency was a high priority of the Rainbow Coalition. Early on in the presidential process, Jackson opened his Iowa headquarters in a small town in rural Iowa rather than at the state capital in Des Moines. He invested a generous proportion of his time in that state, fashioning an economic message which demonstrated his compassion for the family farmer and displaced factory worker alike, irrespective of race. Even though Iowa was a caucus state susceptible to highly motivated voters, as demonstrated by Robertson's finish ahead of Bush, Jackson's vote there on February 8 was less than 10 percent. It was not an insignificant showing in a state with few African-American residents, but he had hoped to do better. (His poorest primary of all was the 5.4 percent he registered later in February in South Dakota; these were the only states that Gephardt carried outside his native Missouri.) In New Hampshire, Jackson's 7.8 percent was only marginally better than his figure in 1984 when his campaign was in the midst of the "Hymietown" crisis. The Jackson goal of double-digit support was already encountering tough going in some parts of white, rural America.

The possibility of a Jackson breakthrough among white voters appeared on the horizon when, unexpectedly, Jackson scored 19.8 percent of the votes in Democratic caucuses held in Minnesota on February 23 and scored 26.8 percent a week later in Maine. Neither state contained a significant number of African-Americans. Minnesota, of course, has been a consistently liberal, strongly Democratic state, home of Hubert Humphrey and Walter Mondale. Moreover, small businessmen and farmers were hurting economically. The Rainbow Coalition there included a well organized and hard-working gay and lesbian alliance (Jackson consistently spoke more directly and more frequently than other candidates on such issues as gay rights and programs for AIDS victims). Jackson's co-chair was a Carleton College professor, Paul Wellstone, who would go on to become the only candidate in 1990 to defeat an incumbent U.S. senator, Rudy Boschwitz.

The Maine caucus was held on a Saturday night and went largely uncovered by the national press. CBS had to abandon its exit polling when half of the caucus sites never even opened. Jackson had traveled there in times past to show support for striking paper workers who returned the compliment by showing up at the sparsely attended caucuses. Volunteer college students helped to pull out Jackson voters in Portland and Bangor. Sensing he might do well, the Jackson campaign bought $10,000 worth of television time for the last two days before the voting. Dukakis, as he had in Minnesota, won the state handily, but the national press never examined why Jackson had done so well. Jackson insiders told me they had decided not to tell the press about the labor-union effort lest they be accused of Mondale-type, interest-group politics.

The Jackson pre-Super Tuesday momentum continued in Vermont, where Dukakis captured a clear majority but Jackson polled another 25.7 percent of the vote. The common denominator of these early Jackson showings in the North was that they took place in states where the electorates were smaller, African-Americans were largely absent, and white residents may have felt correspondingly less threatened.

Jackson Vote Before Super Tuesday

	Date	Turnout	Percent	Winner
Iowa*	Feb. 8	126,000	8.8	Gephardt
New Hampshire	Feb. 16	123,360	7.8	Dukakis
South Dakota	Feb. 23	71,606	5.4	Gephardt
Minnesota*	Feb. 23	100,000	19.8	Dukakis
Maine*	Feb. 23	11,000	26.8	Dukakis
Vermont	Mar. 1	50,791	25.7	Dukakis
Wyoming*	Mar. 1	2,968	12.9	Gore

* Caucus
Source: *Congressional Quarterly*, July 16, 1988.

On Super Tuesday in the South and border states the Jackson share of white voters exceeded 10 percent only in Virginia, Maryland, and Texas and averaged no better than 7 percent of the region as a whole according to network exit polls. The low ratio was confirmed in North Carolina, which publishes registration figures identified by race. Jackson went out of his way to identify with the interests of white families, workers, farmers, and issue-oriented progressives, sometimes at the expense of opportunities to further solidify his black base. Jackson staff in the field talked of trying to raise the "comfort level" of white constituents by avoiding public rallies dominated by black audiences, and the candidate went out of his way to make appearances on racially mixed college campuses in Southern states.

He ran better than his averages in college towns such as Gainesville, Florida; Athens, Georgia; Chapel Hill, North Carolina; and Charlottesville, Virginia; although it should be remembered that large numbers of African-Americans hold service jobs in these communities. Standing by his side in

95

Texas was the state's agriculture commissioner, Jim Hightower, one of the few white officeholders in the region not backing Gore. (Hightower would be defeated by a Republican in his 1990 bid for re-election.) Jackson made his best showings among white voters in the Maryland and Virginia suburbs of the District of Columbia, polling better than 20 percent in Montgomery County, Maryland; and Fairfax County, Virginia. Jackson scored 14 percent among white voters who identified themselves to exit pollsters as "liberal," though Dukakis took 44 percent of that group and did best among all candidates in union households. But Jackson coordinators in Super Tuesday states expressed disappointment over the white turnout for their candidate.

> At a barbecue for Democratic election workers in South Carolina, a white couple grumbled about the "niggers we never saw before who showed up to vote in our precinct."

Conversations between this white observer and white voters in the South confirmed the persistence of racism at the ballot box. The word "nigger," or a swiftly pronounced "nigrah," was used openly in places where shotguns are still visible in the cabs of pickup trucks. At a barbecue for Democratic election workers in South Carolina, a white couple across the table grumbled about the "niggers we never saw before who showed up to vote in our precinct." Well-to-do whites, more inclined to mind their manners, would speak with disdain of Jackson's "presumption" that he should consider himself qualified to be president. "We're not prejudiced, mind you," one said reassuringly, "but it's ludicrous for somebody like that who never spent a minute in government and shouts like a black preacher."

The campaign did attract a number of white volunteers, and conspicuous numbers of whites came to hear Jackson speak. A half-million Southern white voters marked Jackson's name on their ballots only 20 years after the Civil Rights Act. But the ideal of a Rainbow Coalition never burst across the sky.

Nonetheless, in states outside the South which scheduled caucuses or primaries on Super Tuesday, the results were more encouraging.

Jackson Vote on Super Tuesday Outside South

	Turnout	Percent	Winner
Massachusetts	713,447	18.7	Dukakis
Rhode Island	49,029	15.2	Dukakis
Washington*	104,000	34.6	Dukakis
Hawaii*	3,914	37.8	Dukakis
Nevada*	5,048	20.9	Gore
Idaho*	4,633	19.4	Dukakis

* Caucus

Source: *Congressional Quarterly*, July 16, 1988.

The pattern, however, foreshadowed problems ahead. Jackson was making his best showings in Democratic caucuses where turnouts were small rather than in primaries. As the campaign headed toward larger states—Illinois, New York, Pennsylvania, Ohio, New Jersey, and California—where a lion's share of the delegates would be apportioned, those optimum conditions would no longer prevail. Furthermore, in a head-to-head race between Jackson and a dominant white candidate, even though Jackson polled respectable percentages of the overall vote, he would no longer be in a position to register the sort of impact he managed in the three-way battle for the South.

A series of circumstances had denied Jackson a portion of the media credit his Super Tuesday performance should have generated. In Alabama, one of his best states, the computers broke down in Birmingham on election day, so that the magnitude of the Jackson victory was not apparent until television coverage was off the air. The timing of the Jackson sweep in South Carolina, coming four days after Super Tuesday, obscured his achievement of carrying more states than any other candidate and leading the popular vote, too. In Texas, Jackson's delegate strength exceeded Dukakis's in the precinct caucuses held just after the primary, but by then the national press no longer regarded the South as headline news.

All eyes were next on the Illinois primary, where favorite son Paul Simon enjoyed organizational backing across the state because his delegate slate, chosen when Simon seemed to be riding high in Iowa, contained the names of the party faithful, thus diminishing Jesse Jackson's chances of attracting white voters in this crucial post-Super Tuesday test.

Whether Super Tuesday had improved Democratic prospects in November was far from clear. Republicans were ecstatic over Vice President Bush's smashing primary sweep and the turnout of Republican primary voters. The Jackson-Gore-Dukakis contest had satisfied few of the Democratic skeptics who believed that only a moderate nominee could restore party fortunes south of the Mason-Dixon Line. Gore, though not their first choice, had at least survived the first round. He would have to show some staying power in the North as well. Dukakis was a puzzle to most Southerners, but Super Tuesday demonstrated that he now had to be taken seriously as a national candidate.

Perhaps the most important fact was that, despite all the hoopla, two out of every three voters had chosen not to participate at all. It was anybody's guess whether the results on the second Tuesday in March would bear any relation to the final outcome on the first Tuesday in November. The idea that a series of regional primaries might make a more sensible way to nominate a president than a hodge-podge of individual states following a disorganized calendar was not advanced very far by the experience with Super Tuesday. As for the chances of a person of color being elected president of the United States, Jesse Jackson's experience in the once solidly Democratic South demonstrated that there was still a long way to go.

8

If Not This Time, Next Time

Political campaigns by their nature are hectic, disorderly, unwieldy, dispersed, and, more often than not, beset by internal contradictions and tensions. Those who try to harness the beast need a diverse set of skills, not to mention endurance and emotional resilience. Jesse Jackson's 1988 campaign for the presidency was more free-wheeling than most, and the men and women responsible in the field represented an unusual combination of talents.

The coordinators for Jackson in the South were drawn chiefly from Rainbow veterans of 1984, including a growing cadre of African-American state legislators, clergymen who had done battle for civil rights and voter registration, black professionals and businessmen, and whites who had been active in various liberal groups, such as those advocating nuclear disarmament and equal rights for women. In many cases those holding campaign titles did double duty, holding down their regular jobs by day and accomplishing their primary chores at night. Full-time, paid staff were rare and for the most part included receptionists, secretaries, and other office functionaries.

Compared to the competition, the Jackson campaign

organization was modest in size and resources. Governor Dukakis and Senator Gore enjoyed the advantages of being incumbent officeholders. They could raise funds and recruit experts based on reasonable expectations of being the Democratic nominee and, perhaps, the president. Their well-heeled national headquarters, for example, contained separate divisions to handle the schedules of Kitty Dukakis and Tipper Gore. In Massachusetts, Dukakis could order up a computer print-out of the names and addresses of every retiree from the Massachusetts state pension system living in Florida and send it along to campaign aides there. The Gore Senate staff could assemble a roster of every radio and television outlet in Tennessee that broadcast signals into congressional districts in adjacent primary states where delegates would be elected.

Jesse Jackson, 47, already engaged in his second quest for the presidency, would be only 51 in 1992. When the presidential campaign started in the year 2000, Jackson would still be under 60. Nobody had expected him to go so far, so early. Some African-American leaders were both surprised and wary of this controversial personality who had stolen a march to become the best known national political figure of his race. Several prominent rivals had supported white presidential candidates in 1984 and withheld their endorsement of Jackson in 1988. Publicly they were careful to maintain appearances, but privately they expressed their reservations as to whether Jesse Jackson was the right man for the White House, or even the right man to test the waters of black-white coalition politics.

Within the Super Tuesday states, two African-Americans of demonstrated political experience were already preparing to run for governor in the years immediately following 1988—Lieutenant Governor L. Douglas Wilder of Virginia in 1989 and former Atlanta mayor Andrew Young in Georgia in 1990. Neither endorsed Jackson. But the strategy of both would likely be affected by Jackson's showing in their home states, the psychology of success being contagious in politics.

Furthermore, the nuts and bolts of the Jackson field operation would be the nucleus from which to build their own
political apparatus.

Besides Atlanta, African-American mayors already pre-
sided in New Orleans, Birmingham, Washington, D.C., Baltimore, Philadelphia, Chicago, and Los Angeles, all located
in states holding presidential primaries in 1988. The Jackson
national campaign would activate once again these local
constituencies, elevating their political awareness and stimu-
lating the feeling of being part, this time, of a national
movement. New York City, rich in potential Jackson delegates, was also scheduled to elect a mayor in 1989. Jackson's
showing there might be a determining factor for assessing
the prospects for electing an African-American the next year.
Thus, every vote for Jackson in 1988 would serve a dual
function: this time, next time.

While working on a book in 1969 about the participation
of the disadvantaged in the electoral process, I was a firsthand observer of Mayor Carl B. Stokes' re-election campaign
in Cleveland, Ohio. Stokes had been elected in 1967 by only
1,679 votes in a city where voter registration was 62 percent
white and 38 percent black. In winning, he had polled
slightly less than 20 percent of the white vote and an average
of 95 percent in the black wards. Turnout had been around
80 percent among both groups. It was remarkably high for
African-Americans, whose number on the voting lists had
been augmented by an all-out registration drive by the
Congress of Racial Equality (CORE) and by visits from
Martin Luther King, Jr., and aides from the Southern Christian Leadership Conference.

Advisers to Stokes from the faculties of Case Western
Reserve and Cleveland State University crunched the numbers and told Stokes that there was no way he could win
again in 1969 unless he boosted his share of the white vote
without boosting white turnout, since the second time around
registration among African-Americans had dropped. (Black
turnout had also dropped in 1967 between the Democratic

103

primary and the general election; it is hard to sustain momentum among those who are accustomed to feeling "disconnected" from the electoral process.) Stokes, a smooth personality who had worked his way up from service as an alderman, reduced the visibility of his efforts among African-Americans and spent the lion's share of his time reassuring Cleveland's white voters of his mainstream values. He won re-election by 3,753 votes. The total vote throughout the city was down 20,000 from 1967, but Stokes' share of the white vote (turnout down by four percent) increased to 22 percent.

> From Alabama to New York, none of the Jackson coordinators felt they were going through the motions of an exercise doomed to fail.

By an interesting coincidence, Gerald Austin, Jackson's 1988 national campaign manager who had been active in Bobby Kennedy's 1968 race for president, came from Columbus, Ohio. Undoubtedly cognizant of the precedents established by Stokes two decades before, Austin could hardly count on remaking Jesse Jackson into a latter-day Carl Stokes. But the arithmetic had not changed much over the years: African-Americans running in multi-ethnic constituencies against white opponents could count on a rock-bottom nine out of 10 votes from voters of color who came out to vote. The danger to their candidacy was to fail to attract a sizable proportion of white voters or, worse yet, to provoke a heavy outpouring of whites voting their fears in favor of a white opponent.

The inclusive character of the Rainbow Coalition, Jackson's concept of a patchwork quilt stitched together from interest groups too small to prevail by themselves, fitted in with an overall scheme to raise the comfort level of whites with his candidacy. From the beginning no one understood better than Jackson the dangers of polarizing the electorate.

But there was no way to conceal, even if anyone should

want to, the outpouring of black pride in a legitimate contestant for the presidency of the United States. It was there to see any time the television cameras pointed Jackson's way as he worked his way through a crushing, touching, cheering crowd of African-American admirers. How could Jackson possibly make the very core of his symbolism "invisible"? And how could anyone insulate the hearts and minds of Americans watching these triumphal journeys from generations of prejudice?

In the South, Jackson's success on Super Tuesday gave his campaign coordinators the feeling that he would win. They could then pass on the torch to those in the rest of the country in a contest in which pundits were still writing about the probability of a brokered convention at Atlanta. In a key Northern state such as New York, the Jackson planners envisaged coming in first if two or more white candidates were still seriously in the race. Talking to Jackson coordinators from Alabama to New York, it was clear that none of them felt that they were going through the motions of an exercise doomed to fail.* They believed. When the voting was over, they looked back on their accomplishments with satisfaction and pride. They felt part of a process in which the end was not yet in sight.

---

* See Debriefings, page 139, for a full account of interviews with Jackson state campaign coordinators.

9

The Road After Super Tuesday

As the campaign moved North after Super Tuesday, racial polarization continued to thwart Jackson's outreach to sectors of the white community. In the Illinois primary on March 15, Jackson polled only 7 percent among white voters, paying, some said, for his high-profile role through the years in Chicago's African-American community. This was scarcely better than he had done in the racially conscious Deep South. When the votes were counted, he had run second to Paul Simon's 42.3 percent of the vote with 32.3 percent, though well ahead of Dukakis (16.6) and Gore (5.1). Unfortunately, under Illinois' winner-take-all system in congressional districts, Jackson ended up with only 37 delegates to 136 delegates for Simon. (These became a bone of contention when Simon eventually dropped out of the race without releasing them to Jackson. Such incidents prompted Jackson to press for reform of the delegate apportionment system for 1992.)

An unexpected Jackson victory created a stir 10 days later when he won 74 delegates in the Michigan Democratic caucuses against 55 for Dukakis and only nine for Gephardt, who had made an all-out last-ditch effort to revive his candidacy. Here was a seemingly significant triumph in a large industrial state. The caucuses were held on a Saturday night and the results became known too late to be digested by the television networks and Sunday newspapers. But the annual Gridiron dinner of Washington correspondents was rocked by the news that Jackson had won Michigan, transforming him overnight into a presidential possibility who had to be taken seriously.

Among the hardest hit economically of the Rust Belt states, heavily unionized Michigan was particularly receptive to Jackson's brand of populism.

The television networks, discouraged by problems in interviewing participants in Maine's sparsely attended caucuses, had decided to skip Michigan altogether. Reporters who depended more than they liked to admit on exit polls were suddenly without a clue as to what had really happened. Suddenly, newspapers, news magazines, and broadcasters were featuring a showdown between an ebullient Jackson and a faltering Dukakis in the Wisconsin primary on April 5, asking the question: "How far will Jesse go?"

In truth, of the 212,668 Democrats (3 percent of the voting-age population) who had come out to the Michigan caucuses, 43 percent had voted in urban Detroit congressional districts which went 90 percent for Jackson even though Mayor Coleman Young had endorsed Dukakis. (As used to happen in Cook County, Illinois, the returns were very slow in being reported from Detroit, leaving the early impression from caucuses in other parts of the state that Dukakis was ahead in Michigan.) Arab-Americans, politically important in Michigan, had raised substantial funds for the Jackson campaign. Jackson also did well in union strongholds such as Flint and Pontiac where unemployment rates were high, and won in

Kalamazoo and Saginaw. He exceeded the 15 percent threshold for delegates in all 18 House districts. Among the hardest hit economically of the Rust Belt states, and with Gephardt no longer a serious factor, heavily unionized Michigan was particularly receptive to Jackson's brand of populism.

The bubble of euphoria in the Jackson camp burst 10 days later in Wisconsin, where he managed to poll 23 percent of white voters on April 5, but lost to Dukakis by 20 points. Misled by large crowds of curious onlookers, Jackson himself had believed he might carry Wisconsin. "Come alive on April five," he shouted to friendly looking white audiences. He ended up with only 24 out of 91 delegates. He did not do nearly as well as hoped in Kenosha, for example, an automobile manufacturing city where Jackson had paid his dues on the picket line protesting the closing of a Chrysler plant. Dukakis carried Kenosha. That part of Wisconsin was served by Chicago media which through the years had featured Jackson as a controversial figure engaged in racial confrontations. Nevertheless, large crowds had turned out for Jackson rallies elsewhere in the state, which had a minority population of only 4 percent. As in Iowa, he campaigned hard among farmers and received enthusiastic receptions on college campuses.

Correspondents covering the Wisconsin campaign reported that audiences seemed friendly and attentive, contemplating the unprecedented possibility of a black winning the nomination for president. *Newsweek* reported that Jackson "was generating a political electricity that hadn't been seen or felt in years—a populist dream of black and white voters, their spirits kindled, finding common ground under a unifying banner of hope." Between these outward manifestations and the final decision of how to cast their votes, something happened. In the privacy of the voting booths, Jackson lost out. He ran close to Dukakis among Democrats, but the Massachusetts governor benefited from crossover votes, permitted under Wisconsin law, from Republicans and independents who helped him amass 47.6 percent to Jackson's

New York Mayor Ed Koch attacked Jackson for his relationships with Louis Farrakhan and Yasir Arafat and announced that "Jews would be crazy to vote for Jackson."

28.2 in an electorate of more than one million.

The highly polarized New York primary on April 19 was, in effect, the practical end of the road. Jackson won 15 percent of white Democrats (as against only 6 percent in 1984), but lost decisively to Dukakis, 51 percent to 37 percent with 1.5 million voting. The split among Catholic voters went 42-18 against Jackson and 65-6 among Jewish voters after New York Mayor Ed Koch, who endorsed Gore, attacked Jackson for his relationships with Louis Farrakhan and Yasir Arafat and announced that "Jews would be crazy to vote for Jackson."

"We had a game plan for New York," said Hulbert James, state campaign coordinator for Jackson. "We started working on it in January and stuck to it. We executed it exactly as we planned it. About 1.4 million turned out in 1984. In a three- or four-way race we figured 500,000 would win it this time. We made all our targets. But we never expected the white vote which turned out. Whites turned out in some places as if it were a general election. The black vote exceeded our targets. We thought 500,000 would win the state. We got 580,000. We raised a million dollars. But Koch spoiled the message. We could never get on the free media with Jesse's message.

"Jesse's message was *rainbow*. We had no nationality groups in our campaign. We said the same thing to everybody. Jesse didn't want to focus on any one group. But Koch turned the whole attention toward the Jewish question. Nothing else appeared on the media for a week."

The depth of feeling about Jesse Jackson among the Jewish community in New York was unmistakable. Some of it was tied to anti-Semitic speeches by Jackson's old ally in Chicago,

110

Louis Farrakhan. Jackson severed all relationships with Farrakhan during the 1988 campaign but did not "denounce" him as demanded by some Jewish leaders. Some of it stemmed from passionate support of Israel vis-a-vis the Palestine Liberation Organization and its leader, Yasir Arafat, with whom Jackson had been friendly. Black-Jewish relationships in New York City had deteriorated during the incumbency of Mayor Ed Koch, who had opposed affirmative action "quotas," campaigned on a law-and-order platform, and become estranged from African-American political leaders. Festering beneath all these other tensions was the 1984 "Hymietown" incident.

Many Jews in New York (including Koch) had been active in the civil rights movement in the sixties. Others had been in the forefront of the battle for civil liberties during the McCarthy era. In conversations during the New York primary with reporters and editors with Jewish roots whom I had known and admired through those years and since, I was taken aback by the intensity of their antipathy toward Jackson. These were persons with bona fide liberal credentials. They often said they agreed with Jackson's positions on most issues. Nothing in their personal lives stamped them other than as individuals of tolerance and compassion. But they became downright vehement about Jackson.

Before Jackson arrived for the New York primary and before Koch's incendiary pronouncements, there had been discussions within the Jackson campaign staff about how to defuse the "Jewish problem." John F. Kennedy in 1960 had scheduled a televised dialogue with Protestant ministers in Houston to discuss the implications of a Catholic running for president. A New York Jews for Jackson committee was organized, and it proposed a similar meeting between Jackson and local rabbis. The meeting never happened. Jackson, who had performed a *mea culpa* public apology in a Manchester, New Hampshire, synagogue during the 1984 primary, was reluctant to go through that again. Some members of his national campaign staff advised him not to become bogged down with defensive postures.

The Koch-Jackson controversy drowned out other themes in the New York campaign. Race and racial tensions became the dominant themes of talk shows and columnists. On primary day there was an unexpectedly heavy turnout of Democratic voters from conservative, middle-class neighborhoods. "Catholics in Queens, Westchester, and upstate poured out to vote," said Jackson coordinator James. "They heard Koch say Jesse would leave the country undefended and bankrupt the treasury . . . .

"We carried New York City. We doubled the white percentage over '84. We were a dozen points higher overall, 37 percent isn't bad in a state where only one in five residents is black . . . . All this in a situation where we were sandbagged by the media. It was a terrific showing in the state. But Dukakis, with 51 percent, came out the big winner. If Gore had gotten 20 percent, we could have won. The vote for Dukakis became a vote to stop Jackson and the Gore vote flowed to him."

The mood in Jackson state headquarters the morning after Dukakis had carried 50.9 percent was gloomy as field staffers prepared to move on to Ohio and California. The race, they felt, had been lost. Now it was a question of achieving a strong bargaining position within the party when it came time to adopt a platform and choose a ticket.

Gore dropped out of the race after New York, but did not release previously won delegates who might otherwise have been allocated to Jackson. According to CBS exit polls, Jackson's proportion of white votes leveled off at 14 percent in Pennsylvania, 14 percent in Ohio, and 12 percent in Indiana, in what had now become a two-way contest. Even though Jackson won 80 percent of the vote in the District of Columbia, turnout did not exceed 1984 levels and Dukakis took a respectable 18 percent of the total.

As the primary season drew to a close, Jackson polled 38 percent of the vote in Oregon, a state with an African-American population of only 2 percent. Oregon confirmed the phenomenon observed elsewhere: Jackson ran most strongly among white voters where black voters were fewest and posed the least ethnic rivalry over housing, schools, or jobs. Whether this might change as the American people grow more accustomed to the idea of a minority president or respond differently to another sort of minority standard-bearer remains to be seen.

All told, 12 percent (better than two million) of Jackson's total vote in the 1988 presidential primaries came from white voters, according to exit polls. Although that is a very substantial showing in a certain sense, nonetheless when that same two million is compared with the overall total of 17 million white Americans who voted, it is apparent how far Jackson would still have to go to make a Rainbow Coalition become a reality.

The nomination of Michael Dukakis was cemented by victories on June 7 in California (60.8 percent) and New Jersey (63.2 percent). The focus then changed to the choice of his running mate and adoption of a platform at the national convention in Atlanta in July. The long campaign inevitably created tensions between the Dukakis and Jackson camps. The relationship between the two was important, because if the Democrats were to be successful in November, the white and African-American constituencies which had combined to win national elections in the distant past would need to accommodate themselves to some appropriate new form of rainbow coalition.

Breakdown of Communication

The importance of good communication to the pursuit of politics was dramatically illustrated by the breakdown between Michael Dukakis and Jesse Jackson over the selection of a vice-presidential candidate in the summer of 1988. It is not clear exactly what happened and why. The decision of the Dukakis campaign to choose Senator Lloyd Bentsen of Texas was apparently reached at a late-night meeting around

113

A Recap of the Primaries:
How the Democrats Voted

When the percentage (12) of white votes for Jesse Jackson in the 1988 presidential primaries, as calculated by exit polls in 33 states, is applied to the total number of those voting according to official state returns (17 million whites), Jackson's white total exceeds two million.

	Percentage of Primary Voters	Jackson	Dukakis	Others
Total (millions)	22.7	6.6	9.7	6.4
Total Percentage	100%	29%	43%	28%
Men	47	29	41	30
Women	53	30	43	26
White	75	12	54	36
African-American	21	92	4	4
Latino	3	30	48	20
18-29 years	14	38	35	27
30-44	31	36	37	27
45-59	25	30	42	28
60 and older	30	19	53	29
Liberal	27	41	41	19
Moderate	47	25	47	28
Conservative	22	23	38	38
Democrat	72	33	43	24
Independent	20	20	44	34
Catholic	30	18	60	22
White Protestant	36	10	43	47
Jewish	7	8	75	17

Source: *The New York Times*, June 13, 1988. Based on exit polls from 33 states; 10 from *The New York Times*/CBS News, 14 from CBS News alone, five from ABC News, and one from NBC News.

the kitchen table in the Dukakis Brookline residence, attended by Dukakis himself, Susan Estrich, his campaign manager, and other key aides. Bentsen was at his Georgetown residence, asleep with his phone off the hook. Jackson was on the campaign trail in Cincinnati.

One might have expected the Dukakis campaign to be sensitive about announcing the Bentsen selection in a manner that would not offend either Jackson or the seven million voters who had picked him over Dukakis in the primaries. It would be elemental, it would seem, to make sure that Governor Dukakis personally informed Jackson of his decision before it became known to the general public or reporters.

As it turned out, Jackson learned from reporters that Bentsen was the vice-presidential choice when he disembarked from his plane the next morning in Washington, D.C. It was a humiliating experience for him. Jackson delegates scheduled to attend the forthcoming Democratic convention in Atlanta expressed deep-felt anger over the seemingly gratuitous insult to their standard-bearer. For a time, the rift threatened Democratic hopes for a harmonious convention. Only extraordinary efforts by the Jackson leadership at the convention patched together a semblance of harmony, and it is fair to say that the incident carried over into a campaign in which Dukakis polled smaller margins than needed among African-American voters.

In seeking to explain away the failure of Dukakis to reach Jackson in time, Dukakis aides provided the press and others with an elaborate scenario. First, it was disclosed that when it was discovered that Bentsen could not be reached by telephone the night of his selection, it was decided to wait until morning to convey the glad tidings. When the way was finally cleared to clue in Jackson, no one near Dukakis could find Jackson's telephone number. (It had been turned over to Paul Brountas, chief Dukakis fund-raiser, but failed to make its way to Susan Estrich.) When contact was finally made with the hotel at which Jackson was staying in Cincinnati, he had already left for the airport to catch a flight to

Washington. Thus, it was explained by the Dukakis campaign, the governor never managed from his State House office to get through to Jackson before he was confronted by reporters as he left his plane in Washington. Jackson learned from them for the first time that Bentsen had been selected, and could not conceal his surprise. If this scenario is to be believed, it suggests a rudimentary incompetence within the Dukakis campaign staff.

When it was discovered that the Bentsen phone was not answering, it would have been a simple matter to find a Georgetown neighbor to go over to the Bentsen residence to inform him that the governor was urgently trying to reach him. It is hard to imagine a politician objecting to being awakened to learn that he had been picked as the vice-presidential nominee. Failing that, the urgency for setting up a plan to relay the news to Jackson as soon as possible after notifying Bentsen would seem obvious to most political practitioners. How could that be carried out? The quickest, most confidential and efficient means would have been a message via the Secret Service detachments assigned to both parties: "Peso wants Pontiac to call soonest."

(The choice of code names assigned to the candidates by the Secret Service is revealing. John F. Kennedy was called "Lancer." Peso alluded to Spanish-speaking Dukakis's reputation for squeezing a nickel. Pontiac, used to describe Jackson, has its roots in an old, redneck racist joke: "What's a Pontiac? Poor Old Nigger Thinks It's A Cadillac." The Secret Service is allowed to play such games on its own if nobody in authority objects.)

Since nobody thought of a more direct means, it required no leap of ingenuity to figure out a way to communicate with the Jackson plane in flight. Failing that, someone might have been dispatched to board the aircraft immediately upon arrival before the passengers began to debark.

As none of these alternatives was executed, one can conjecture that charges, later during the campaign, of chaos in Boston had a solid basis in fact. Or might there be a different explanation? Flushed with their primary victories and annoyed with Jackson's claims to consideration, it might well have been that Dukakis and his advisers simply felt no compunction to accord the runner-up any special consideration. It is not unknown within the mores of Boston pols to give the back of the hand to losers. Nor has the Boston Democratic establishment been noted for its sensitivity toward African-Americans. The Dukakis campaign at that point might simply have decided to flaunt its independence from Jesse Jackson and his supporters. (No one has yet confessed to either explanation.) That kind of arrogance would indeed be political error, but error of a different order. We may never know the truth of the matter. But either way, the results were ultimately damaging to the Dukakis cause.

Strenuous efforts by Jackson and his convention manager, Ronald Brown (later to become Democratic national chairman), managed to soothe some of the resentments among the more than 1,000 Jackson delegates in Atlanta. Compromises were hammered out on the platform to accommodate the goal of the Dukakis forces to avoid positions thought to be unpopular with mainstream voters. There was an enthusiastic public showing of party harmony and goodwill between the primary rivals. But seeds of mistrust lingered.

Census reports on the voting turnout in November 1988 indicated that 4 percent fewer African-Americans voted for president than in 1984. Voting was down by 50,000 in three Chicago congressional districts and down by 30,000 in Baltimore. Such defections undoubtedly contributed to the Democratic candidate's losses in such must-win states as Illinois, Ohio, Pennsylvania, Michigan, and California. The white-black alliances which had produced off-year senatorial victories in North Carolina, Georgia, and South Carolina did not materialize in 1988. African-American voters in the South who had made a crucial difference in these contests had not poured out even for Jackson in the Super Tuesday primaries. Their apparent disillusionment with national politics was compounded by the relative indifference of the

Democratic presidential campaign to the Rainbow agenda. Compared to 1984, presidential voting fell off by 12 percent in heavily black Jefferson County, Mississippi, and by 10 percent in Lowndes County, Alabama, and Greene County, Georgia. The Dukakis-Bentsen ticket failed to carry a single Southern state and lost by such margins that African-American voters could not have saved the day. The ambiguous character of the Democratic ticket coupled with its failure to cope with the negative attacks from the Bush campaign could share the blame for the debacle.

One school of thought concerning the future of the national Democratic Party in the South argued that it could afford to alienate black voters if it could regain the traditional allegiance of blue-collar and middle-class whites. Some African-American strategists maintained that the time had come not to be taken for granted within the party. The new Republican national chairman, Lee Atwater, announced that the GOP would make the wooing of African-American voters a top priority. Super Tuesday and Jesse Jackson's candidacy, on the one hand, had raised the level of expectations among African-Americans everywhere. Jackson's ultimate defeat in the primary process, however, had caused an inevitable let-down.

Discussion among pundits turned to the question of whether the protest politics generated by the civil rights movement could be successfully pursued on the national scene or whether a more subdued style (modeled after Virginia's L. Douglas Wilder or Mississippi Congressman Mike Espy) was the most effective route for equal opportunity at the polls. Jesse Jackson epitomized the former. In the wake of Jackson's substantial but insufficient showing in 1988, a new generation of African-American candidates for high office at the state and congressional levels emerged to build on—and transcend—the Jackson legacy. Meanwhile, Jackson himself gave every indication that he was keeping his options open for 1992.

10

The Jackson Legacy

Jesse Jackson's campaign in the 1988 presidential primaries had an impact far beyond the 1,167 delegates pledged to his candidacy at the Democratic National Convention in Atlanta.

As the front-runner in total number of delegates won on Super Tuesday, Jackson forced both the media and the Democratic Party for the first time in history to focus on the presidential candidacy of an African-American.

As a politician, Jackson exhibited his charismatic appeal to millions of American voters at a time of disillusionment with the ability of candidates generally to demonstrate either personal appeal or qualities of leadership.

In comparison with the resources thrown into the campaign by his two principal rivals—Governor Michael Dukakis and Senator Albert Gore, Jr.—Jackson achieved phenomenal results in terms of the crowds attracted to his campaign appearances and regular exposure in the mass media. The low-budget Jackson primary campaign benefited from his acute instincts for publicity, the enthusiasm and dedication of his core African-American constituency, and his success at raising issues that transcended racial lines.

Jackson focused public attention on a roster of "progressive" issues not articulated as strongly by other candidates or actually avoided by those seeking to cast the Democratic Party in a "moderate" or "conservative" image. In the primary debates, he put forward for the first time the issue of American corporate responsibility for the loss of jobs to overseas plants. He emphasized the impact of Reagan administration policies on trade policy, defense expenditures, and relations with Central America, South Africa, and the Middle East, as well as on the economic well-being of workers and farmers. He reached out to families of all races across the country with his expressed concerns, and he proposed programs on health care, education, the protection of the environment and problems of the elderly. His detailed position on controlling drugs and the passion he brought to the subject prompted suggestions of creating a special position of anti-drug czar for him if the Democrats won the election. At the very least, he helped place the drug problem on the national political agenda.

While recognizing popular concern with drugs and crime, Jackson emphasized the importance of dealing with the causes of antisocial behavior in our society instead of focusing exclusively on punishing the offenders at great cost to the taxpayer. He made specific proposals for cutting the national debt by encouraging allies to bear a larger proportion of overseas defenses and simplifying the roster of expensive weapons systems. He took an unequivocal position in favor of sanctions against South Africa and its policy of apartheid, including the release of political prisoners such as Nelson Mandela. These coherent, agenda-setting positions gave the Jackson candidacy credibility, making it more difficult to dismiss the idea of a black president as a merely emotional expression of racial pride.

Jackson's candidacy, including the image of a Rainbow Coalition, was an attempt to advance the ideal of an integrated society. There has been disagreement within the African-American community over whether the nation is prepared to support power-sharing among all the elements of a diverse society. All told, 12 percent of the 17 million whites who voted in the 1988 Democratic primaries voted for Jesse Jackson—or slightly more than two million. Not a bad start, yet it was crystal clear that the millennium was not yet at hand. The proportion of Southern white voters on Super Tuesday willing to vote for a black presidential candidate was not very large, yet it was double the percentages four years before. Such "progress" is painfully slow, but in times past Catholics and Jews contesting for political office managed to build on modest levels of preliminary acceptance.

After winning the New York primary against Ed Koch with conspicuous support from Jackson, David Dinkins kept Jackson at a public distance from his general-election campaign.

Jackson managed to win significant proportions of the white vote in states where the number of African-Americans was small enough not to provoke anxiety about residential neighborhoods, school populations, or job opportunities. In large urban states, Jackson's share of the white vote was substantially larger than in 1984. Jackson's ability to increase whites' comfort level with African-American candidates for high office was important to the long-run evolution of the political process. But as a lightning rod for controversy himself, Jackson was handicapped in trying to defuse racial polarization. An eloquent and powerful advocate for finding the common ground, he was also perceived as a difficult and arrogant loner. The two Jacksons competed for space in the media and created cross-pressures in the minds and hearts of the voters.

In the long run, Jesse Jackson's 1988 campaign for the presidency left a legacy which had a pronounced effect on the future efforts of African-Americans to win office all over the country.

Ronald H. Brown, Jackson's floor manager at the Atlanta

convention, subsequently became the first African-American elected to be national chairman of the Democratic Party.

Once Jackson carried New York City in the April 1988 primary, the feasibility of an African-American candidate for mayor in 1989 had been documented. David Dinkins, the African-American Manhattan borough president, previously reluctant to run, entered the mayoral race and unseated incumbent Ed Koch in the Democratic primary, using the identical precinct targets and the same field organization responsible for Jackson's strong run the year before.

Ironically, Dinkins' candidacy also benefited from the Jackson experience in New York by avoiding the pitfalls which hampered the latter. Dinkins went out of his way to reassure Jewish voters by reminding them that he had publicly denounced the views of Louis Farrakhan and by promising unequivocal support for the state of Israel, positions not taken by Jackson.

In the general election against the Republican-Liberal candidate, former U.S. attorney Rudolph Giuliani, Dinkins' cool and cautious demeanor was a sharp contrast to Jackson's hot, evangelical style. After winning the primary against Koch with conspicuous support from Jackson (who spent primary day making get-out-the-vote appeals from black radio station WLIB), Dinkins kept Jackson (with his acquiescence) at a public distance from his general-election campaign. While reasserting his private friendship, Dinkins took care to emphasize to the press that he, not Jackson, would be calling the shots in a Dinkins administration.

The pride and energy of the African-American community, which had been stirred by Jackson's two campaigns for the presidency, manifested itself by giving 95 percent of its votes to Dinkins, who at the same time polled roughly 30 percent among white voters, including Jews. Like Jackson, Dinkins carried the city by a narrow margin, but in this instance in a constituency including the whole electorate. The image of a Rainbow Coalition, as defined by Jackson, had become a partial reality.

> The troops who had delivered banner African-American pluralities for Jackson in Richmond, Surrey, and Hampton Roads performed once more for Wilder.

As the first African-American mayor of the nation's preeminent city, David Dinkins, who had been Jesse Jackson's New York campaign co-chairman in 1988, assumed a place in a new generation of African-American political leaders, different in temperament, perhaps, and more moderate in their approach to issues than the pioneering spirit. But their link to the Jackson legacy was unmistakable.

In Virginia, where Douglas Wilder became the first modern African-American governor in the country, the Jackson legacy played out in a different fashion. Be it remembered that Jackson's 45 percent in the 1988 Democratic primary in Virginia was his highest in any state, although then-Lieutenant Governor Wilder had remained aloof. Be it remembered that Jackson had polled a significant minority of white voters in the fast-growing suburbs adjacent to Washington, D.C. Building on the infrastructure put in place by the Jackson campaign while fashioning his own image as a conservative, mainstream Democrat who happened to be black, Wilder carried the Old Dominion by a razor-thin margin (fewer than 7,000 votes) and ran well behind white Democratic candidates for lieutenant governor and attorney general. The troops who had delivered banner African-American pluralities for Jackson in Richmond, Surrey, and Hampton Roads performed once more for Wilder. Wilder also replicated Jackson's penetration of white voters in the Northern Virginia suburbs adjacent to Washington, D.C. And he did better than Jackson among whites in the more conservative areas of the Old Dominion.

Like Dinkins in New York, Wilder in Virginia enjoyed the benefits of the African-American electorate first mobilized by Jackson while adding a cushion of white voters by standing apart from too much identification with the Jackson personality—the best of two worlds.

A key factor in the success of both Dinkins and Wilder against their Republican opponents was their capitalization on an issue which Jackson almost alone among Democratic presidential candidates in 1988 had dared to emphasize: a woman's freedom to choose whether or not to have an abortion. Both Republicans Rudolph Giuliani in New York and Marshall Coleman in Virginia came into their campaigns strongly identified with "pro-life" anti-abortion positions. A Supreme Court decision in early 1989 had opened the way for abortion rights to be determined at the state level, and President Bush had vetoed a bill passed by the Democratic Congress which would have continued federal funding for abortions for victims of rape and incest. Dinkins and Wilder, without going any further than to question the role of state government to limit women's freedom to choose, made themselves more attractive to pro-choice voters than their Republican opponents, both of whom seemed oblivious to poll data showing a large number of women who said that the issue would be an important factor in their decision at the polls. What had been considered an example of Jackson's injudicious pursuit of issues turned out to be one of the keys to enabling white voters, including Republicans, to throw their support behind other Democrats, white and black.

The Politics of Race

The dilemma confronting any African-American candidate for public office in this country in white-majority constituencies is how to turn out a solid core of black voters without turning off the white voters necessary to achieve a winning coalition. There is no such thing as yet in the United States of America as a colorblind election.

The enduring factor of race at the polls was specifically documented in a book by Professor Thomas F. Pettigrew of the University of California, Santa Cruz, and Dr. Denise A. Alston, a former public policy fellow at the Joint Center for Political and Economic Studies in Washington, D.C., analyzing Los Angeles Mayor Tom Bradley's two campaigns in the eighties for governor of California (*Tom Bradley's Campaigns for Governor: The Dilemma of Race and Political Strategies,* Joint Center for Political Studies, 1988). Using statistical regression techniques to analyze a variety of possible factors in those contests, Pettigrew and Alston concluded that race played a "significant negative role."

The authors pointed out that despite Bradley's qualifying experience as mayor of Los Angeles, combined with a non-threatening, non-controversial demeanor, "a critical portion of the white California electorate was 'not ready yet' for a black governor, no matter how reassuring he or she might be." Race in American politics, Pettigrew and Alston observed, "serves as a political lightning rod that attracts political energy whether the candidates intend to or not."

In his first campaign, Bradley led his white opponent, George Deukmejian, in the polls by seven percentage points, with seven percent saying they were still "undecided" in the last weekend of the campaign. Bradley eventually lost by 93,000 votes out of more than 7.3 million cast. The same phenomenon of leading in the polls by margins far larger than the actual voting results was experienced in 1989 by Douglas Wilder in his narrow win in Virginia and David Dinkins in New York City. Political consultants generally estimate that an African-American running against a white opponent should concede all the "undecided" voters in such polls, owing to the reluctance of white voters to admit openly their negative feelings about black candidates. When racial symbols are used in a campaign, as in the Republican 1988 Willie Horton ads or North Carolina Senator Jesse Helms' anti-affirmative action ads used in 1990 against African-American Harvey Gantt, they release highly charged political energy against the target.

Jesse Jackson's more controversial personality made him

more vulnerable to white backlash than other African-American politicians like Bradley who, despite their lower-key campaign style, could not escape the drag of race. However, he did much better in mobilizing his core African-American constituency than Bradley, whose attempt to present a reassuring image to white voters was encumbered by the perception among black voters that he was taking their support for granted. Bradley won 42 percent of white voters in 1982, but the turnout of the majority against him was heavy. He won 95 percent of the African-American vote, but the turnout among this massive bloc was comparatively light. This combination spelled defeat for Bradley. Jackson did much better at bringing out African-Americans to the polls but came nowhere near matching Bradley's showing among whites. The arithmetic of race turned out no better for Jesse.

The delicate balancing act between charisma and moderation worked for David Dinkins and Douglas Wilder in local constituencies where they already were well known, and where African-Americans had been recently mobilized by Jackson's 1988 primary campaign for the presidency. Whether such success will be lasting or transferable to the national scene remains to be seen.

In outlining the political strategies available to African-American candidates, Pettigrew and Alston issued three warnings on how to counter racism in the campaign and how to relate to both African-American and white constituencies. Although Jesse Jackson waged his 1988 campaign for the presidency before these guidelines had been published, it is instructive to measure his efforts against them.

First, Pettigrew and Alston cautioned that African-American candidates must develop a campaign strategy to counter the often subtle, but still powerful, appeals that tend to surface whenever blacks run against whites. Jackson indeed suffered from white backlash even though his Democratic opponents for the most part took pains to avoid appeals to racism. The political lightning rod of race is operative regardless of intent.

Jackson did most poorly among white voters in those states (North and South) where a large African-American population triggered white fears or was perceived as a potential threat to white values. In New York, Mayor Ed Koch's direct attacks on Jackson while endorsing Senator Al Gore were followed on primary day by a large turnout for Dukakis in white Catholic precincts where racial tensions already existed.

Jackson's special problems with Jewish voters magnified this white backlash. Jackson's own racial remarks directed at Jews in previous campaigns were underestimated as a factor that needed to be dealt with dramatically in formulating 1988 strategy. This handicap was compounded by Jackson's outspoken support of a Palestinian homeland in the Middle East, whatever the merits of this position as an argument for peace.

The personal antagonism among some Jews toward Jackson was deep, unforgiving, and persistent. It extended beyond rank-and-file voters to Jews holding key positions in the national media and Jews who are ordinarily important sources of campaign funds for Democratic candidates. Many of them have been close friends of mine during my lifetime spent in journalism and politics. When I told them I was doing a book about Jackson, it usually triggered a heated discussion. These hostilities seemed largely focused against Jackson as an individual, rather than against African-American candidates generally, although there is evidence in large, urban areas such as New York City and Chicago of Jewish fall-off from normal Democratic pluralities when African-Americans head the ticket.

Pettigrew and Alston's second point concerns how African-American candidates should approach African-American constituencies. Candidates cannot assume the support of minority blocs but must work actively for a strong minority turnout. There is evidence that Jackson did not maximize the potential of African-American voters in some key states, although the loss of potential turnout came nowhere near that of Tom Bradley's 1984 campaign. Jackson had concentrated on registering new African-American voters in 1984 and that effort paid off for white Democratic Senatorial candidates in the South in 1986. His 1988 rainbow campaign of inclusion, however, deflected much of his energy and resources in other directions.

> African-American candidates must walk a tactical tightrope: they must actively mobilize minority voters, yet not appear so militant as to seem threatening to a broad range of moderate white voters.

The problem of limited voter participation by African-Americans is part of the larger general problem of steadily shrinking turnouts in presidential elections. Studies show that it is the less educated, young, poor and transient segments of the population who register and vote in the smallest proportions. Because African-Americans figure prominently in all these demographic categories, the black vote is more vulnerable to the overall downward trend in participation. If Jackson's charismatic appeal to black brothers and sisters could not inspire a massive African-American turnout, does that mean that a substantial number of disadvantaged Americans, defeated and demoralized by the harsh realities of limited opportunity, have given up on the electoral process? Aside from racial pride in successful, local African-American candidates, there is unfortunately little concrete evidence that their election has vastly improved the quality of life for the disadvantaged residents of problem-plagued inner cities such as Newark, Philadelphia, or New Orleans.

Finally, Pettigrew and Alston describe the tactical tightrope that African-American candidates must walk: they must actively mobilize minority voters, yet not appear so militant as to seem threatening to a broad range of moderate white voters in a still race-conscious society. In states where Jackson did best among his African-American constituency, he paid the price among white voters. Although he improved his 1984 showing among white voters in the Deep South on Super Tuesday, he could not break through the 10-percent mark. He carried New York City, but fared poorly in the suburbs.

The balancing act African-American candidates must perform is sometimes cited as an example of how the white majority in this country seeks to control by conferring leadership status on blacks it finds acceptable and vetoing those not deemed acceptable. Furthermore, the balance requirement only goes one way, because recent white Republican presidential candidates have shown that they can win sweeping elections while advocating policies which have been, to say the least, insensitive to black needs. African-American voters are usually forced to choose between two white males.

Jesse Jackson is often characterized by white pundits as too militant, too divisive or lacking the appropriate governmental experience. However, even when an African-American with a more cautious style comes along, one like David Dinkins or Douglas Wilder—men who paid their dues to the party with long service in local or state government—the establishment press usually allows them only a short honeymoon. Dinkins has been taking his lumps for New York City's budget problems inherited from the policies of white predecessors. Wilder, after a euphoric beginning, has undergone a relapse since he authorized a committee to test the possibility of a place on the national ticket. Even before the rift between Wilder and Virginia's Senator Chuck Robb hit the headlines in the summer of 1991, *The Washington Post*, once an ardent Wilder admirer, began to portray him as a cynical revisionist who has been tailoring his positions to the winds of opportunism. "Wilder Feints Left, Then Right as He Spars for '92," a front-page headline declared on April 4, 1991. "Supporters Never Know Which Wilder Will Show Up," the headline continued inside.

The future of African-American candidates in national politics is part of the internal debate within the Democratic Party as to their best strategy for retaking the White House in the last decade of the 20th century. As ideological positions are being staked out within the party ranks, Jesse Jackson is cast as part of the left-of-center wing of the party that has advocated policies which, some claim, are anathema to moderate white voters who have been defecting to the Republicans.

The impact of the 1988 Jackson campaign not only manifested itself in the subsequent election of Dinkins and Wilder the very next year, but also in the election of African-American mayors in cities with a majority of white voters: New Haven, Connecticut, Kansas City, Missouri, and Seattle, Washington. A sea change was taking place in American politics, characterized by a proliferation of African-American candidates on state and local tickets. It was not yet the millennium, however, as Jackson's own shortfalls in his quest for the presidency illustrated. In 1990, Harvey Gantt, who had previously been beaten for re-election as mayor of Charlotte, North Carolina, would become the first black nominee for the U.S. Senate in the South since Reconstruction. He would lose to incumbent Republican Senator Jesse Helms, whose polarizing campaign would result in a heavy turnout of white voters. In South Carolina, State Senator Theo Walker Mitchell (who had led the Jackson caucus in Precinct 12 in Greenville) won the Democratic primary for governor. He would lose by more than two-to-one to incumbent Republican Governor Carroll Campbell, who had led George Bush's overwhelming 1988 primary victory. In another Super Tuesday state, Georgia, former Atlanta mayor Andrew Young would seek to separate himself in 1990 from the politics of black protest by coming out for the death penalty and subordinating social issues to programs for economic development to attract new business. One result was a disappointing low turnout of African-American voters in the Democratic primary, where a white opponent, Lieutenant Governor Zell Miller, would defeat Young handily before going on to victory in November. An African-American businessman, Kenneth (Muskie) Harris, would defeat a Ku Klux Klan sympathizer in the 1990 Republican primary for lieutenant governor in Arkansas, although white supremacist David Duke would poll 44 percent in his race for the U.S. Senate in neighboring Louisiana. In the North, an African-American Republican, Gary Franks, would win an open congressional seat in a Connecticut district where black residents constituted only a minority of the population.

Some pundits interpreted the victories by Dinkins and Wilder to be signs that Jesse Jackson's days as the most prominent African-American figure on the national stage were over. Democratic national conventions would no longer be required "to keep Jesse happy." Other voices would be available to talk for the idea of minority participation in a multi-ethnic society in tones more appealing to mainstream American voters.

Political observers, not necessarily friendly, urged Jackson in 1990 to run for mayor of Washington, D.C., where he had amassed better than 80 percent of the vote in each of his presidential primary runs. In a situation where there would be limited federal funds to attack problems of housing, education, and drugs, and where congressional committees exercised considerable power, Jackson chose not to avail himself of this "opportunity" for experience in governmental office.

With typical Jackson derring-do, he focused instead on championing the goal that the District of Columbia become a full-fledged state within the Union (when it might then elect Jesse Jackson to the United States Senate) and ran for the newly created post of non-voting shadow senator. Meanwhile, he continued to circulate his views by means of a syndicated newspaper column and television talk show, and the presidency of the National Rainbow Coalition, Inc.

Speculation as to what Jesse Jackson might do in 1992 began the day after the 1988 election was over. The national press tended to dismiss his prospects, much as it had done after 1984 and continuing right up to Super Tuesday in 1988. The conventional wisdom, expressed by television commentators and newspaper columnists and reinforced by the spectacular military victory in the Persian Gulf, was that the Democratic Party had little chance, in any case, to unseat George Bush. Among Democrats themselves, many argued that, in order to win, the party had to steer a more moderate course.

The 1990 midterm elections did little to confirm the argument that Democrats had to be more like Republicans in order to win.

Only in this way could the party win back the middle-class Democrats who had defected to Reagan and Bush because of their aversion to government initiatives which allegedly cost too much, benefited only the poor and minorities, and didn't work anyway. In addition, liberal Democratic presidential candidates who opposed capital punishment, favored women's right to choose whether or not to undergo an abortion, or were skeptical of U.S. constitutional authority for prayer in the public schools were said by some self-styled moderate Democrats as well as conservative Republicans to be at odds with the basic values held by a majority of Americans.

If this theory were true, even a white candidate taking the positions Jackson held would have no chance. Add to that the issue of race, and a Jackson candidacy was seen as sure to divide potential Democratic voters and afford the Republicans a field day to exploit racial fears as they had done before. Wouldn't it be wonderful, this school of thought suggested, if Jackson did the decent thing—accept the credit for breaking political ground and leave the field to a new generation of Democratic politicians?

The 1990 midterm elections did little to confirm the argument that Democrats had to be more like Republicans in order to win. Andrew Young sought crossover votes by emphasizing economic development by Georgia business rather than economic opportunity for the disadvantaged and was beaten badly in the state Democratic primary for governor. Diane Feinstein came out for capital punishment in California, but lost the governorship anyway. Ann Richards won Texas against a conservative Republican, admittedly a poor candidate, with the backing of a liberal coalition of women, teachers, minorities and unions. Down-the-line progressives won a Senate seat for the Democrats in Minnesota and defeated a Republican congressman in Vermont. Republican Senator Jesse Helms did indeed turn back Harvey Gantt in North Carolina with the help of television ads suggesting that Gantt would favor quotas taking jobs away from working whites and giving them to unqualified blacks. But the North Carolina legislature subsequently elected an African-American as speaker of the house for the first time in history.

The Republicans readied the "quota issue" for the 1992 national campaign by a last-ditch fight against a Civil Rights Bill formulated to undo Supreme Court decisions restricting the government's power to prosecute employers who discriminate against minorities in the work place. There seemed little doubt that the GOP was banking in 1992 on racial symbols (*á la* Willie Horton) to tap into voters' anxieties about race. In these circumstances, it was argued, a Democratic ticket led by Jesse Jackson, or including even a less threatening African-American such as Douglas Wilder, would be made-to-order for white demagogues campaigning in the grassroots.

Jackson's Own View

Jackson himself said he felt no pressure to declare his intentions for 1992 early. Interviewed by telephone on May 28, 1991, Jackson said that if he ran, "I think I could get 10 million votes in the Democratic primaries and 1,800 delegates." That would still be less than the more than 2,000 required for a majority, but more votes than Dukakis polled in the 1988 primaries.

Looking back on 1988, Jackson said, "After we won in Michigan, I think the Democratic Party organizations in other states focused on beating me. It wasn't so much that they were listening to what Dukakis or Gore had to say. In Wisconsin and New York, they said, 'A vote for Gore is a vote for Jackson.' I couldn't do anything to stop the racial code for giving Dukakis a vote. If Gore had remained a viable candidate, I think the outcome might have been different." Asked if he had to do it all over again, would he have done anything different, Jackson's answer was "No."

The key to his 1988 campaign, Jackson said, was "building coalitions. The more we made the case for the small farmer, the case for the working man who had lost his job to an overseas plant, for a woman's right to free choice, for economic justice regardless of gender or race, the better the coalition. I think we recognized the growth dimensions of building coalitions. The better the coalition, the more we scored. I received more white votes in 1988—two million—than any black in history, in this country or any other."

To the direct question of what he thought the legacy of his two campaigns for the presidency might be, Jackson replied: "One of the more significant things we did, when I reflect back on it, was breaking out of the mold of American politics. There was a noose around our necks, and the rope kept getting tighter and tighter, that somehow blacks are not equal, that women are not equal. So in presidential politics we were always choosing between two white males.

"In 1984 I made the case from New Hampshire to California that if a woman could hold the top office in Israel and India, why not the United States? One result, I think, was to make a contribution to the nomination of a woman, Geraldine Ferraro, as the Democratic vice-presidential candidate. One day a woman will run for president. One day an African-American will win the nomination.

"The idea of considering a Colin Powell, Bill Gray or Doug Wilder for top national office is one of our victories. The fact that their names are included means that an artificial ceiling is being removed. The American people have gotten used to the idea of watching an African-American debating the big issues which affect all segments of the population."

Jackson said that the eye-opener for him on the need to challenge and broaden the political process was when Harold Washington ran for mayor of Chicago in 1983. "Ted Kennedy came in and Walter Mondale came in to endorse the organization's candidate against Washington. We pleaded with them as national leaders not to come in, but they did it anyway." Jackson made up his mind then and there that African-Americans would have to take on the white power structure in the Democratic party in order to escape the racial noose.

"I didn't see myself as a presidential candidate. I just thought that there ought to be an African-American who would run for president and I was prepared to do all that I could to help that candidate. My first appeal was to Maynard Jackson. I thought he had all the qualifications: he was a first-rate lawyer, he was a community leader, he had been mayor of an important city, Atlanta. He didn't want to run. I talked to Andy Young. He wasn't ready to run either. People kept raising the idea that 'Jesse should run. Run, Jesse, run.' Somewhere along the line I got thrust into becoming a candidate." The rest, as they say, is history.

A major part of his legacy, Jackson believes, was the registration and activation of new African-American voters who have become "a new force in American politics." He recalls that "when I ran in the Democratic presidential primaries, we never had the support of the traditional party organizations. Our initial victory was in 1986 when we registered two million new African-American voters. What happened? Four Democratic senators were elected in the South who polled only a minority of white voters: Sanford, Fowler, Shelby, Breaux. The Rainbow Coalition vote was a determining factor in three other states: Florida, Maryland, and California. The black vote was responsible for the Democrats recapturing the Senate and all those Democratic committee chairmanships today. We elected a lot of young people to state office in '86 too. The big turnout among the young foreshadowed the 1988 primaries."

Jackson doesn't think it is inevitable that progressive Democrats scare off middle-class white voters. He argues that the majority of Americans of every race have the same needs as African-Americans.

> **"I'm not going to forsake my quest for soul for the White House, although I don't believe they are necessarily mutually exclusive. If the Democrats are not willing to fight for the high moral ground, to fight for racial justice, then I am ready to keep hope alive."**

"The common ground that unites poor blacks and working and middle-class whites in this country are economic issues. The need of working whites for economic reforms is being diverted by appeals to race. The small white farmer is not losing out to black farmers. The manufacturing jobs that are moved abroad are being taken away from both whites and blacks. The Reagan tax-budget shifts came out of the pockets of the white middle-class. Reagan's 'welfare queen' was a phony issue used to justify a tax cut for the wealthy. We need to reinvest in America. When the president talks about a new world order, we must ask: Who is included? Today, Kuwait is in worse shape than urban America. In two years, Kuwait will be rebuilt. But two years from now, if we continue without a plan of investment and renewal, urban America will be worse off.

"Republican politicians need a decoy. Race is the decoy. I had to go double duty in my campaign to make the case for common ground and, at the same time, shoot down the racial Scud missiles. The Democratic Party must be fully prepared to fight race-baiting, to meet manipulative fear campaigns head-on.

"The trap in 1992 is for the Democrats not to fight for racial justice. The Beltway analysts who say that racial justice only turns off white voters are forgetting history. In 1960 here was a white Catholic guy who worried about Martin Luther King, Jr., in an Albany, Georgia, jail. The Democrats lost in 1968, not over race but over the Vietnam War. Carter in 1976 stood up for racial justice. He was perceived by African-Americans as an honest Southerner who would reach out to them. The Democrats have been too slow in standing up to George Bush on Willie Horton or his red-herring arguments against a Civil Rights bill."

If that sounds like a candidate talking, Jesse Jackson in the spring of 1991 had obviously not yet made up his mind. "White voters say to me: 'Jesse, if you were white, you'd be president. Be patient with us.'

"Right now my interest is as much in the soul of America as in the White House. The soul of America has been corrupted by race-baiting, by sex discrimination, and all the code words poisoning the political atmosphere. I believe it is imperative to seize the high, moral ground. We must draw a line against the current rise of hate crimes, racism, anti-Semitism, crimes against women. As people feel the walls close in on them, they turn on each other.

"I'm not going to forsake my quest for soul for the White House, although I don't believe they are necessarily mutually exclusive. The Abolitionists fighting slavery had the moral center. The occupants of the Warsaw Ghetto were the moral center against Hitler. The marchers to end wars were part of the moral center. If the Democrats are not willing to fight for the high moral ground, to fight for racial justice, then I am ready to keep hope alive."

Whatever his future, the road to Super Tuesday and beyond had established Jesse Jackson as a historic landmark

"Keep Hope Alive!"

on the American political scene, "keeping hope alive" for the time when tolerance levels would make possible the election of African-Americans not only to high local and statewide office but one day as president of the United States.

Interviews With Jackson Campaign Coordinators

Alabama State Senator Michael A. Figures
Jackson Co-Chair

I was busy in the legislature during the campaign, so couldn't spend as much personal time as I would have liked. But you don't need that much of a structured campaign for someone like Jesse Jackson. The Jackson campaign is an extension of his own personality. He is one of the best himself at using the media in his own behalf. His support in the state was simply *entrenched*. The people were just waiting for the chance to go out and vote for Jesse. Jesse had been to Mobile five or six times since 1984. The media didn't understand the *depth* of Jesse Jackson's candidacy in the South.

We had the vice president of the AFL-CIO as a co-chair. The state employees association was behind us. Jesse had gone underground with the mine workers. He came to Mobile and walked the picket lines with ship workers. The Birmingham bunch had gone with Mondale four years ago.

Black voters don't like conflict among the brothers. They stay away from the polls. I know. I've been through it. This time Mayor Arrington hosted a rally for Jackson, and that was it. Once he told the system, once he gave the signal, that was it. In '84, Arrington told everybody to go his own way. Not this time. So he went to Egypt on the day of the voting. That was long planned. It didn't make any difference. Jefferson County went 60 percent for Jackson (in Green County it was 86 percent)—nearly three times the Gore vote. Gore spent a ton of money on television, Jesse less than $5,000 in Birmingham. We spent less than $20,000 in the whole state—virtually nothing.

The people in the national campaign always have their own idea, their own judgments. They kept scheduling Jesse where he could talk to white voters. We might have used him better up in the Black Belt—bringing out the vote we already knew we had. He just couldn't get to Mobile again, so we may lose a delegate there by 100 to 200 votes. The only trips Jesse ever made to Mobile were to talk to white groups. You have to be careful you don't alienate your support base. National said he just couldn't get to Mobile again. I told them to go ahead and cancel Mobile. The red-neck types in Mobile got on TV to back Gore.

But once the Alabama Democratic Caucus people in Montgomery got on board, teamed up with our New South Coalition, that was it. It was completely different than in '84. The whole system was for Jesse. We didn't have to do anything. Jesse got his own message across, across-the-board. The voters walked in on Super Tuesday.

If Super Tuesday had no other impact, it gave Alabamans the feeling that they were participating in a national election. There was a national aura about the thing. Here's a black guy who could make it, who could win it all. We would have had a field day beating up on Nunn. I don't think this country will elect two presidents from Georgia. A Nunn can get 15 percent to 20 percent of the black vote, no matter what, but that wouldn't work against Jesse. The voters are attached to

Jesse like kids are attached to Michael Jackson: charisma. Everybody underestimated his resilience after '84. Over in Atlanta, Coretta King doesn't control any votes. She's an intelligent woman, but that's all. To the average person on the street, they think: why aren't these black people supporting a black guy? Seems self-serving.

The white vote for Jesse in Alabama was disappointing. I haven't been able to check it out yet, I noticed that in Weston county, which has no blacks, Jesse got about 38 votes. There *is* a white vote for Jackson in the South. The exit polls may underestimate it. In Alabama, a white man is not particularly anxious to volunteer publicly that he is voting for a black man. Where there is a substantial black population, whites still feel 'It's them or us.' One paper ran a story warning that there are no black maids in Massachusetts.

Don't know yet about the turnout. I think it was higher this time in Mobile than '84. We made some mistakes probably. The *Birmingham News* said there was some complacency because all the black politicians were backing Jesse this time; four years ago there was a lot of competition between the two camps. The long, paper ballots here are confusing. There were a large number of absentee ballots, and we're not sure they all got counted. There are still racial problems with respect to voting in some parts of this state. And, of course, the computers broke down. The media are always trying to stir up trouble. The headlines this morning are saying "Jackson and Gore in Dead Heat," and now we're hearing on the radio that Jesse finished seven points ahead.

Fred Gray, Alabama Democratic Caucus

We're an arm of the Democratic Party, an autonomous arm. We endorse candidates in primaries; the party does not. We supported Mondale four years ago, because he was the clear front-runner and was more electable. This time the black community was unified. Jackson has matured. He is more broad-based. He is not strictly geared to a symbolic, personal showing.

Political players like . . . Figures have their own agenda. The New South Coalition is mostly made up of people in the state legislature. The black ministers give plugs in the churches, but don't need to be operational. We're a grass-roots organization. We have networks in over 60 counties. Since Jackson didn't have any street money, we relied on volunteers. We distributed sample ballots, absentee ballots, set up transportation for primary day. But I think there were more walk-in votes this time than usual. But we used the resources of the state organization and local folks to get out the vote.

We had little contact with the national Jackson organization. Here in the Second District, Jackson will get four out of the five delegates, and we endorsed all four. The New South Coalition endorsed a different set of delegates, but ours were better known, more active. The women we endorsed were educators, active in the party. We endorsed two elected officials and one former office-holder.

I don't know about the white vote. There were a lot of Gore supporters out there who thought Gore was a realistic choice to carry the conservative South in November. I think the white vote hinged on the unknown factor of the 'comfort feeling' with Jesse. You would need the precinct box returns for all the white boxes to know for sure. Maybe there would be one or 2 percent, maybe 5 percent.

The young of both races are the toughest to get involved. The young are just not plugged into history. The Alabama Democratic Caucus has focused most of its energy into trying to win more black elected officials. We have launched 185 suits in Alabama to get fair black representation in local government and have settled 160 of them. We are going to check out those who crossed over to vote in the Republican presidential primary to prevent them from voting in the Democratic primary later this year. You can't have it both ways. We're going to expose them. We're going to monitor the process and ask for access to the sign-in sheets. I don't

Interviews

think Alabama will split the presidential and statewide primary again. It makes for misunderstanding and probably hurts turnout.

Georgia State Senator Gene Walker
Jackson Co-Chair

I'm surprised that everybody else is surprised by how well Gore did in Georgia. Eighty percent of the state's elected officials endorsed Gore, including the governor, Senator Sam Nunn, and Speaker of the House Tom Murphy, who is the most powerful man in the legislature. After Murphy endorsed Gore, House members started wearing Gore buttons. Governor Harris's and Senator Nunn's endorsements were last-minute, and they may have not been all that enthusiastic. Everybody respects Nunn, black and white. Nunn seems fair-minded. He gets good press. He has not brought shame to the state. But we'd have whipped Nunn on Super Tuesday if he had ever become a candidate.

Congressman John Lewis endorsed Jesse in a big news conference. Lewis definitely made a contribution. He gave his support at Ebenezer Baptist on the Sunday before Super Tuesday. He had been hesitant for a while, because he expected to be a super-delegate. I don't know where Andy Young comes from. He thinks he is the only black who can get elected where the majority is white. If Martin Luther King was the problem, Andy would have forgiven Jesse by now. I think it's jealousy. Jesse's star shines brighter than his star. John Lewis held back because Gephardt was a colleague of his in the House, not because of any worry about Jewish opinion in Atlanta. If you associate with Jesse, you can improve relations with the Jews. The best way to do it is to become involved. The fact is, Jesse reached out to make Austin his campaign manager.

Maynard Jackson co-sponsored a fund-raiser, but he was not as active as he was in '84. I talked to Young twice myself. Eugene Duffy, who managed Julian Bond's campaign, sponsored an important fund-raiser. Young helped us somewhat, but never showed up anyplace personally. He never overly hurt us, but he didn't do enough. He used the excuse that he was the host at the national convention.

I wrote my doctoral dissertation on the history of the Southern Christian Leadership Conference. Jesse tried to do something for SCLC when it was immobilized by King's death. Now they try to diminish him. I don't buy that. Martin, Sr., held no grudges. I don't think that the aftermath after Martin's death has anything to do with Jesse's problem in Atlanta. That's not the real cause—it's emotions of envy and jealousy.

The talk about experience, or Jesse's supposed lack of it, is not germane. The captain of a ship can be president, but he doesn't need the detailed knowledge of a navigator. He has to be able to make judgments, understand the components, try to synergize these things. Nothing offends me more than the talk that Jesse lacks experience. If people don't know better, they should. Reagan wasn't elected because he had been a governor. He was elected because of his ideology, the tenor of the times, his meanness about 'keeping niggers in their place.' His philosophy was clear: Reverse the civil rights gains; annihilate the Communists. Reagan appealed to the basest phobias: the fear of Black Takeover and the Red Scare—nothing to do with experience.

Jesse had a different message–reaching out, the patchwork quilt, opportunity for everybody. The American people should understand that Jesse is providing them with the greatest service, like Abe Lincoln did in abolishing slavery. Jesse is liberating our minds. Jesse is forcing people to entertain the notion that a black man can be president. It's a process. We can't lose. If not this time, next time. Look how long we had slavery. This is only Jesse's second time. He's a lot younger than Reagan.

There will be great opportunities for persons who can co-opt his themes: (1) stopping drugs, (2) creating jobs in the U.S., (3) stop exporting jobs abroad, (4) strong defense, but not to excess, (5) homes for the homeless, (6) health care, (7) education. We need commitment to these problems in a humane way. Get some specifics on how to carry these programs out. We want to win. We don't want to scare anybody. We're going to have some black folks dealing with Bush. A humane approach as opposed to Reaganomics. Jesse says he want to reverse Reaganomics. We're going to whip George Bush. All it will take is hard work and organization.

For Super Tuesday I selected Ellen Spears and Mike Mears as co-chairs. Their skins were different, but they shared the same philosophy as Jesse. They were credible and respected. Mears, mayor of Decatur, had thrown some hints that he would like to help out, even though he represented a suburban, white constituency. Mary Young Cummings, a black representative from Albany, was the fourth co-chair. That made it two men, one black and one white, and two women, one white and one black. People like Billy Young downstate kept it going. Billy was one of my stars. I'm 53 and I never met a person as naturally good and unpretentious, totally committed to the rainbow concept. Billy was the main man in carrying the 8th Congressional District. The 8th was one of six we targeted in Georgia. And we carried it.

We didn't recruit as many white workers in the campaign as we would have liked. It's difficult. The *Atlanta Constitution* was a big disappointment to me. Ralph McGill used to write about the way the nation should be. The present *Constitution* wrote about what *can't* be done instead of what *should* be done.

The *Constitution* assigned a white, female reporter to write their main profile on Jesse Jackson. She would go around and talk to anybody who had something negative to say about Jesse. That became the gospel. What supporters had to say was ignored. The negative became the norm. Some white lady complained about her pay when she worked for Jesse's campaign last time. That came out 'Jesse's mean to all people who work for him.' After the voting on Super

Tuesday, whose picture was on the front page? Al Gore's. "Gore makes it 3-man Democratic race," "South has its say: Gore, Bush like what they hear." Jesse had earned the right to be on the front page of the paper. He got 40 percent in Georgia to Gore's 32 percent. He got 27 percent across the whole South to 26 percent for Dukakis and 26 percent for Gore. They gave the play to the man they hoped would win.

I was scared to death when the speaker and all his lieutenants came out for Gore and the paper was massaging the news. I never thought Gephardt would come close. He didn't have anything in the state except Congressman Jenkins. We had the best organization.

We set up a command post in Atlanta with significant labor support from the civil service union. They gave us a phone bank with someone down from Washington to supervise it. We were in contact with all the targeted congressional districts. We had a designated person checking the polls hour by hour. We had 50 vans in the metro area. If voting was down 10 percent somewhere in Fulton County, we sent out the vans with loudspeakers and volunteers to help pull out the voters. A.F.S.C.M.E.—my favorite union—set up a true command station on the sixth floor of the Trust Company bank building.

We had no money. It was truly a people's campaign. We rented headquarters downtown on Peachtree Street for $2,500 a month. We shared it with the Southern regional staff for Jackson. Ron Daniels, Jesse's regional coordinator, was responsible for letting us know when Jesse would be available. We always were glad to see Jesse come. Glad to see him go. It's just too much of a headache to have to explain why he doesn't show up someplace he is supposed to be. Walt Bellamy was in charge of all security activities.

We set up Jesse's appearance at Ebenezer Baptist for the Sunday before Super Tuesday on a week-and-a-half's notice. Actually, the biggest crowd was at the Chapel Hill Harvester Church, Bishop Paul's congregation, where there are three or four thousand every Sunday, more white than black. The black churches, of course, were our primary sources of support. But we always wanted Jesse to be in a black-white context whenever possible. We worked him hard—sent him to a white Catholic church in Cobb County, too.

I think we got some white votes. I can't prove it. I don't know who has the genius to figure that out. How many black voters voted for Gore? Nobody asks them. Blacks aren't monolithic. They always want to know how many whites voted for Jesse. They never ask how many blacks voted for the white candidates. Blacks should realize they are where they are because of Jesse. But some are uninformed how they got there. At least Nunn did vote against Bork, so he must have realized where some of his votes came from.

Michael Mears, Mayor of Decatur, Georgia Jackson Co-Chair

I am the mayor of a city of 20,000, 65 percent white. I think my white constituents supported my involvement with the Jackson campaign, though not voting for him. I ran for re-election three weeks after I endorsed Jesse and received 85 percent of the vote.

We had a group that worked from sunup to sundown. If people are inspired, they will work. If they work, it will show results. Priscilla Painter of the *Atlanta Constitution* says Maryland and North Carolina were better organized, although Jesse lost both. We targeted the districts where we thought we had the best chance and won them. Nunn's endorsement of Gore may have been tepid, but Gore is an attractive candidate. His TV ads stressed national defense, and that's a visceral, emotional issue in Georgia. I didn't see a lot of support for Dukakis. I didn't see any signs of movement toward him in the Atlanta suburbs, although I think he hoped to make a dent there. Jackson finished far ahead in DeKalb County. It's an affluent, eclectic area.

Our percentages among white voters were not earth-shaking, but we showed progress over '84. Jackson had

147

strong support on the University of Georgia campus at Athens in Clark County. We expected that. Young people like Jesse. We found additional support among liberals grown up since the '60s in Savannah, Columbus, and Atlanta. Strong civil rights supporters are with Jesse. We were able to mobilize additional white voters—7 to 10 percent in some districts. We carried about 9 percent statewide.

Jesse did not do so well among blue-collar voters in spite of the help we got from the labor movement. We had the tacit endorsement of the members and leadership of the Teamsters union. If we didn't win acceptance among white voters this time, we won their tolerance. That's a plus for the future. My role now is to help coordinate the Jackson delegates at the convention, keep 'em in line. The delegates will follow the leadership of the Reverend Jackson. I don't anticipate any problems with that. They'll want what Jesse wants.

Bruce E. Lightner
North Carolina Jackson Campaign Manager

I was involved in the Jackson campaign in '84, and I made it clear from the outset that I wasn't going to get involved again unless steps were taken this time to eliminate the chaos. This time was vastly different. We started with a plan to target the key districts in North Carolina. We took pains to involve everybody in the first stages of the campaign. We made it very clear that we wanted North Carolina to be a model state. We asked anyone who was interested to be members of the steering committee. We established lines of communication early. I spent a month of traveling, letters, and phone calls before we officially started. Representative Daniel Blue agreed to serve as Jackson state chairman. He had been for Mondale in '84. There is a natural resistance for anybody to give up power. We said, "Here we come. We want to join hands and work together."

The Rainbow Coalition Committee made the decision in April 1987 to have our convention somewhere in the South. We had a good rainbow in 1984–10 percent. So having Jesse make his announcement here in Raleigh at the Rainbow Convention in December put us in the spotlight. When the leading state officials came out to endorse Gore in January, that was a blow. Especially Terry Sanford, a sitting U.S. senator. At the very least, we expected Sanford to stay neutral. He wouldn't be in the Senate today if it hadn't been for black votes in '86. The lieutenant governor and probably the next Democratic candidate for governor came out for Gore. Jim Hunt came out for Gore. There's a day of reckoning in the future coming due on those accounts.

The clergy had been crucial in '84, especially for fund-raising. We had planned a Super Tuesday Sunday in February to raise money. People For the American Way put out a press release up in Washington raising questions about soliciting campaign contributions in church. That scared off about 85 percent of the pastors.

I had told national we needed $500,000 for a television and radio budget. We ended up spending $16,000 on four spots in Winston-Salem, Raleigh, Greensboro, and Charlotte. And we lost the state to Gore by 8,000 votes.

We stuck to the rest of our plan as best we could. We had a transportation network for primary day, equipped with portable two-way radios to send the cars where they were needed most. The unions gave us some help with phone banks, but unions are not strong in North Carolina. Our target was 31 delegates, and we won 30. But of course we wanted to win the state. We were just overpowered in the last four days.

Sanford and Hunt played things close to the vest until the week before Super Tuesday. Two mailings for Gore went out to every Democrat in the state, addressed by computer, at $87,000 a shot. It would cost us $22,000 for a bulk mailing to black voters, but we didn't have the money. We raised about $50,000 during January and February and national sent back down $47,000. That was the budget.

I knew Ron Daniels, who headed up Jesse's Southern campaign, from organizing the Rainbow Convention. We were in accord on balancing between all-issue appearances for Jesse with pitches to the black groups. Jesse came into the state half a dozen times after announcing.

Jesse's trip to the East Coast to show his sympathy for the fishermen in a jam because the red tide had killed off the fish was my idea. Jesse took a boat out of Wilmington and held a press conference on the problem out at sea. Candidates foam at the mouth for free media like Jesse drew on that. It symbolized Jesse's interest in working men's problems, whatever their race. Two days after Jesse's trip we got a call from a food bank saying they could send food to the fishermen if we could supply the transportation, four tons of it. We asked the truckers to carry it, and they agreed. We didn't hold a press conference about that. But we carried Pender and Brunswick counties this time, where we ran third in '84. And we lost New Hanover by only four votes, where we also ran third four years ago. In Lumberton, where there are Indians as well as the two other races and a great deal of tension, we solidified a lot of possibilities. We carried Robeson County, polling more then 8,000 votes; we lost it with 6,000 in '84.

After New Hampshire, Austin sent a group of six young people who had been working up there. Three went on to work in Florida. They came with a fax machine, something I didn't have. I called them the "Hampshires." They worked hard. It was good to see such commitment to Jesse from white folk. They would send out flyers, get releases out, help with the peace groups and the other progressive groups around the state. Vee Stephenson, who was our office manager, had a lot of good contacts there. We gave them a list of our county coordinators where there were soft spots in our organization. They got along fine with everyone. Steve Canzian, a kid from California who had been living in New Hampshire and working for Gary Hart, is still with the campaign. He's going into New York and California; he lent a hand in South Carolina. I'd like to show you a letter he wrote me: 'Thank you for letting us all get involved without politics and turf battles. Thank you for trusting us.'

I'm not sure how all the votes went, but you could see rainbow walk in the door of our Raleigh headquarters. A white maid at one of the local hotels, a white construction worker, they came in to volunteer.

We had a major disappointment the last weekend before Super Tuesday. All the candidates were scheduled into Raleigh for the state party's Jefferson-Jackson day dinner. There was a tense moment when we found out Jesse couldn't make it. He was stuck in Washington, because the pilot of his chartered jet had flown the limit that day and couldn't bring him down to Raleigh. There were 3,000 at the dinner and it was the major political story in the papers all over the state. Jesse went to Atlanta the next day and ended up in Texas for Super Tuesday. We didn't mind. There had been a lot of emphasis on Texas. National thought they might take it.

We did all right, but we sure wanted to win. We were disappointed that Dukakis and Gephardt didn't do better. Gore spent more than half-a-million on TV and the western part of North Carolina is part of the Tennessee broadcast market. We thought Gore had started slipping when the Democratic machine pulled out all the stops. North Carolina is still one of those states where the organization amounts to something. They saw they needed some direct action and they provided it.

John T. Flannery II
Jackson Co-Chair and Coordinator
for Northern Virginia

Jesse and I were pals from way back. I ran for Congress from the 10th district in 1984. Jesse helped me win the primary against the organization. When he asked me to help, I thought that if a white person stepped forward it

151

could make a difference. We met at the National Press Club in Washington in December, and I got involved in December.

We need a political agenda in Virginia. Virginia politics is pretty laid back. We need an infusion of issues. Jesse has a way of feeling something, then expressing it. The network in the 10th Congressional District was reluctant at first. The issue-oriented people resisted. But they began listening to Jesse on the issues, and they liked what they heard. The nuclear freeze people came aboard. The labor leaders didn't swing in behind—Virginia is a right-to-work state any-way—but they freed their members to go where they wanted. I think Jesse got support from middle-class people filling out their tax returns and finding out they owed more money under the new tax laws. I think his support cut across age lines.

Organization costs money—for index cards, phone calls, all that sort of stuff—and we didn't have much money. We depended pretty much on word of mouth. We had a system of highly motivated workers who have been around for 20 years. Politics isn't seasonal with them; it's year 'round. We needed whites to come forward, first; then to talk to other people to get the word around; and, finally, to motivate people to come out to vote.

Jesse came into the state on short notice. He hit Richmond, Charlottesville, and Northern Virginia. He had already been to Norfolk. Bishop Willis in Norfolk had summoned black people in 1984: "The hands that picked cotton can now vote for a black presidential candidate." He had a much more sophisticated operation this time, though there wasn't much money. He is vice chair of the state Democratic party now and has more organizational politics going. Doug Wilder's absence didn't hurt all that much. He wasn't with Jackson in '84 either. Gore got all the endorsements, but he didn't get much practical help. Jackson was really the only candidate in Virginia with a base remaining from 1984.

On two days' notice we decided to schedule Jesse into George Mason University. It was in the middle of Fairfax

County and provided a mostly white audience. There was a packed house of 900. We were in the business of finding people who didn't know him, then let Jesse speak to them. We picked up 50 volunteers after that rally. It got big media coverage, all affirmative. It came just after the Bush-Rather go-around. Can you imagine how much Bush would help us?

Jesse won 25 percent in the 10th Congressional District, which is only 6 percent black; he polled 29 percent in the 8th, which is only 10 percent black. He averaged 26 percent across Northern Virginia. He beat Gore in all those places, although Dukakis won big in all the Washington suburbs—Maryland as well as Virginia. Jesse's numbers far outstretched the numbers of blacks in an area where people pay attention to government, pay attention to the policy issues, and are not hung up on the question of race. I think there was a minimum number of Republican crossovers, trying to create mischief. You had to be pretty much out in the open in Virginia to pick the Republican ballot. We got a big bang for the buck in Virginia. We won Norfolk and Richmond big and even carried Charlottesville. But Northern Virginia is the story of what is possible to happen in America when voters focus on the issues.

Hulbert James
Coordinator for New York State

We had a game plan for New York. We started working on it in January and stuck to it. We executed it exactly as we planned it. We made all our targets. But we never expected the white vote which turned out. Whites turned out in some places as if it were a general election. The black vote exceeded our targets. We thought 500,000 would win the state; we got 580,000. We raised a million dollars. But Koch spoiled the message. We could never get on the free media with Jesse's message. Jesse's message was *rainbow*. We had no nationality groups in our campaign. We said the same thing to everybody. Jesse didn't want to focus on any one group. But Koch turned the whole attention toward the Jewish question. Nothing else appeared on the media for a week; there was no reporting of the campaign on the media. And Koch got a free ride until almost the end.

There didn't seem to be any national strategy on anything, including the Jewish question. It was the Gary Hart scenario all over again. We weren't prepared for success: We came out of Super Tuesday with no national strategy. It was just on to Illinois, and then the next state, and then the next. I think we could have won New York with a national strategy— and Pennsylvania and surely Ohio, where Austin had run campaigns before and where there were pockets of double-digit unemployment and a substantial black vote. Jesse's message was absolutely right for the Rust Belt. Look at Michigan.

Everybody was down after New York. The candidate was dead tired. Jesse began saying he is running the campaign himself. I know something about that. I worked for Jesse in Washington on voter registration in '84. One thing Jesse is not is a good detail man. Especially when there is a strategy vacuum.

Our basic game plan was to split up the state by geographical areas and by constituencies. We targeted five areas. Tier One were the Big Five congressional districts in New York City: two in Brooklyn, one in Queens, one in Manhattan, and one in the Bronx, where there were the biggest minority populations and which we had carried in 1984. Tier Two were 11 congressional districts where Jesse had won more than 15 percent four years ago; 15 percent was the threshold for qualifying for a delegate. Tier Three were 18 congressional districts within striking distance of electing a delegate. We won delegates in 31 of these 34 congressional districts. We met our goals.

We split the state up into 10 areas covering New York City, Long Island, Westchester, and upstate. We had a full-time office and organizer in each. We designated 15 constituency groups and assigned full-time staff to the black clergy, labor, and students. Others were assigned to the elderly, Latinos, Asians, Jews. Yes, we had a Jews for Jackson group organized from the beginning, but when the national campaign hit town, they never made contact with that constituency except for Jesse's appearance before the Association for a Better New York and a luncheon late in the game which included Peter Straus and others. The word was: we'll talk about issues to everybody, not single issues to issue-groups. The one exception was a rally organized by the gay and lesbian constituency in Greenwich Village and that was one of the best rallies of the New York campaign. Gerald Austin and Ann Lewis were the chief advisers to Jesse on how to handle the "Hymietown" problem, and the word was that they didn't want any appearances with Jewish persons who wanted to talk about just Israel and Farrakhan. Jesse himself didn't want to do that either.

Our coordinator for all of Long Island was the vice chairwoman for the Democratic Party in Nassau County, and she was Jewish. When Jesse kicked off the final campaign in New York, he stopped the first night at a black church in Brooklyn and spent all of the next day on Long Island. The first stop had to be in Brooklyn. But we hoped the press would notice that Jesse was spending that critical first day talking to mostly white voters on Long Island. On election day, the voters in Great Neck voted for Jesse's opponents in record numbers. The turnout of white voters in Ted Weiss's Manhattan district was unprecedented for a primary. But it wasn't just Jewish voters. The Catholics in Queens, Westchester, and upstate poured out to vote. They weren't voting for Jesse. They never heard Jesse's message. They heard Koch say Jesse would leave the country undefended and would bankrupt the treasury. We never expected to do very well with Jewish voters in New York anyway. We were in a no-win situation there. Koch just inflamed prejudices already there. I wondered sometimes whether Koch's performance wasn't part of a plot organized by Dukakis people.

Our game plan was undone by the white turnout.

About 1.4 million had turned out in '84. In a three or four-way race we figured 500,000 would win it this time. Of course, in January we didn't foresee that it would shake down to just three and that Gore would do so badly as the third. If Gore had gotten 20 percent, we could have won. The vote for Dukakis became a vote to stop Jackson, and the Gore vote flowed to him.

There were three main differences between 1988 and 1984. This time the Rainbow Coalition in New York was real. We had the largest delegation at Raleigh. We had a white lawyer as our organizer in Syracuse and won two delegates there. Arthur Eve worked for four years around Buffalo. Fund-raising this time was outstanding. We raised over a quarter-million from young black professionals in a drive organized by Carl McCall. We raised $250,000 in January and hit $500,000 in March. We raised $125,000 in one fund-raiser in Wall Street. David Dinkins raised a million over a period of years for his race for borough president; we raised a million in three months. And this time the role of labor was critical. Labor was with Mondale in '84. When Stanley Hill of District Council 37 committed to Jackson, that was a signal. We had a labor rally attended by 5,000 in the Javits Center and everybody paid 20 bucks to get in. We sent another signal when the Jackson headquarters was located in the headquarters of Local 1199 of the Hospital, Drug and Health workers union. We had biweekly meetings with labor leaders from the beginning. If you look up Eighth Avenue you will see a huge Jackson banner hanging outside the offices of the Hotel, Restaurant and Bartenders Union. Barry Feinstein of the Teamsters went on television after Koch to say "I am as Jewish as Koch and I am for Jesse Jackson."

There were the usual misunderstandings between national and the state campaign. After going from city to city all over the state in a place like Wisconsin, they couldn't understand scheduling a whole day for Jesse in Brooklyn. We expected to get one-fourth of our total vote in Brooklyn.

We had Jesse lined up with an invitation to march up Fifth Avenue in the St. Patrick's Day parade. It was just after Super Tuesday and a second-place finish to Simon in Illinois. He would have been cheered by onlookers at that parade, and it would have happened a month before the primary vote in New York. It would have been a major New York media story. National had scheduled him instead into an affair for Arabs in Michigan. He didn't come. No other candidate came for the parade either. That would have made it even better.

We produced a schedule four weeks in advance for the primary run-up in New York. We planned one area per day in New York City, so the traffic wouldn't kill us. When national came to town, they kept inserting added starters. We planned one afternoon so that Jesse could take his shoes off and get some rest. They stuck in a couple of press conferences, and Jesse got no rest. And the press conferences muddied up the story we had hoped for that day. The reporters made their own agenda.

We planned a half-day in Queens for Jesse to concentrate on the drug problem. We wanted him to stop off in a housing project near where drug dealers had killed a policeman a few days before. The idea was for Jesse to talk about how he cared about the white cops who lost their lives in the drug war. He was supposed to go on to York College and speak to students as a presidential candidate who cared about drugs. Well, the first stop was a meeting of black clergy at a church in Congressman Flake's district. That was okay, but the national press people barred the media from the meeting, starting the day on the wrong foot. The buses then went to the project all right. But nobody mentioned the cop killed nearby and Jesse made no speech about white cops. Oh, there was a great turnout at the housing project and the evening news had one more story showing Jesse in a housing project full of black faces. We didn't need to go to South Jamaica to win votes in those projects. Then an extra stop was added at a drug rehabilitation project where the director had come out early for the local officeholder. So the speech at York College was cancelled. To cap it off, the press buses rolled to a restaurant so that everyone could listen to a fund-raiser for minority building contractors while everybody else ate.

New York was the first time Jackson had any money to spend on television. So what did they do? They hired Spike Lee who is an absolute genius at making movies which appeal to black audiences. The TV spot was in black-and-white and showed Jesse in a three-piece suit walking down the middle of a Harlem street as if he had no idea why he was there. There was something about drugs in the sound track, tailored to black audiences. He also walked down a street in Tarrytown in the same commercial, but the audience had no idea what he might be doing there. There was no time to test the commercial. It was shot on Monday and hit the air on the Thursday before the primary. There were so many com-plaints over the phone that the ad had been pulled by the weekend. Five hundred thousand dollars down the drain. No strategy.

In fairness, there's no complaint about the backing we received in New York from the national campaign. We knew back in January that New York would come at a crucial time. Jesse was here to open our headquarters in January. National came in every two weeks after that. I think they thought they were going to win Illinois. Their expectations soared after Michigan. Jesse spent some crucial time in Colorado just before Wisconsin on the theory that he might win Colorado. It didn't pan out. Wisconsin was a letdown, coming just before New York. But there was no letdown in the campaign here. Jesse doubled the amount of time he spent four years ago campaigning upstate. He went to Buffalo twice. We had big crowds there and in Syracuse.

We carried New York City. We doubled the white per-centage from '84. We were a dozen points higher overall; 37 percent isn't bad in a state where only one in five residents is black. We carried a clear majority of the Latino vote. We won

36 percent in Suffolk County. We polled more than 100,000 upstate. We won 88 delegates. All this in a situation where we were sandbagged by the media. It was a terrific showing in the state.

But Dukakis, with 51 percent, came out the big winner as far as the horse race is concerned. There's no getting away from the feeling of disappointment. Jesse didn't feel like coming down on primary night for the longest time. It was a let-down, no doubt about it. Now I'm here paying off the bills.

Acknowledgments and Sources

I am indebted to my colleague and mentor Charles V. Hamilton, Wallace S. Sayre Professor of Government, Columbia University, for encouraging me to write this book and contributing ideas. Eddie N. Williams, president of the Joint Center for Political and Economic Studies, offered valuable support to this project and accepted it for publication by the Joint Center Press.

The staff of the Joint Center, including Dr. Milton Morris, vice president for research, and Nancy Stella, director of communications, gave aid and guidance along the way. I am also grateful for the contributions of Linda Williams, Marc DeFrancis, and Tyra Wright. Sandy Horwitt edited a draft and suggested changes which markedly improved the text.

My wife, Julie Ellis, added her professional skills as reporter and editor to my own efforts, accompanied me on the travels involved in covering Super Tuesday with tender, loving care, and bore with me during periods of frustration.

The responsibility for what is written is, of course, entirely mine. When one spends many years as a practicing journalist, teacher, and political junkie, one picks up all sorts of information and impressions that cannot be specifically documented. Many of my sources are directly quoted, but many more are not. I thank them all.

A complete bibliography would be too cumbersome, but I found two books especially worthwhile: *Free At Last* by Margaret Edds (Adler & Adler, 1987) and *Politics and Society in the South* by Earl Black and Merle Black (Harvard University Press, 1987). I also benefited by reading, "The Southern Presidential Primary: Regional Intentions with National Implications," by Harold W. Stanley and Charles D. Hadley, in *Publius, The Journal of Federalism*, summer 1987; and a transcript of the Super Tuesday Summit held by the Democratic Leadership Council in Atlanta, June 22, 1987.

I talked to many television, newspaper, and magazine correspondents who covered the Super Tuesday campaign. Particularly helpful were Michael Oreskes of *The New York Times*; Wilbert Tatum of the *Amsterdam News*; Jeff E. Schapiro of the *Richmond Times-Dispatch*; Tyler Whitley of the *Richmond News Leader*; April Witt and Margaret Edds of *The* (Norfolk) *Virginian-Pilot*; Rob Christensen and Ferrel Guillory of the *Raleigh* (North Carolina) *News and Observer* (as well as librarian Colline Roberts); Dwight L. Morris and Jane O. Hansen of the *Atlanta Constitution*, the latter a former student of mine at the Graduate School of Journalism, Columbia University.

I imposed on former students at every opportunity. Among them: Marilyn Milloy, Atlanta bureau of *Newsday*; Addie Rimmer, *Wall Street Journal*; Reginald Stuart, Knight-Ridder Washington bureau; Ben Davis, National Public Radio; Paul Mason, John Quinones, and Linda Pattilo, ABC News; Frances Hardin and Patrick Buchanan, CNN; Robert Kur and Don Oliver, NBC News; Susan Spencer, Mel Lavine, and Brian Healy, CBS News; Otis White, *Georgia Trend*; Lisa Hammersly and William B. Arthur, Jr., *Charlotte*, (North Carolina) *Observer*; Peter Leyden, *Birmingham* (Alabama) *Post-Herald*; Mary Voboril, *Miami Herald*; Bridget O'Brian, *New Orleans Times-Picayune*; Mark Kilpatrick, *San Antonio Express-News*; Jack Ehn, *Albuquerque Tribune*; Howard Maniloff, superintendent of schools, Vance County, North Carolina, formerly of the *Charlotte Observer*; Tom Goldstein, Dean of Journalism, University of California, Berkeley, formerly of *The New York Times*; Nannette Asimov, *San Francisco Chronicle*; Michael Powell, Robin Reisig, Marie Cocco, Edna Negron, and Ellis Henican, *Newsday*; Wayne Barrett, *Village Voice*; Charles V. Bagli, *New York Observer*; Joyce Shelby, *New York Daily News*; Howard Fineman, Shawn Doherty, and David Gonzalez, *Newsweek*; Jerry Buckley, Theodore Gest, and Joseph Shapiro, *U.S. News & World Report*; Richard Duncan, *Time*; Alan Ehrenhalt, *Congressional Quarterly* and *Governing*; Susan Golden, Peter Kerr, David Pitt, and Lydia Chavez, *The New York Times*; Eric Pianin, Neil Henry, Richard Cohen, and Dorothy Gilliam, *The Washington Post*; Helen Winternitz, Douglas Birch, and Eileen Canzian, *Baltimore Sun*; Idris Abdul-Ghani, *Philadelphia Inquirer*; Richard Higgins, *Boston Globe*; Joseph Rodriguez, *Hartford Courant*; John Nichols, *Toledo Blade*; and a host of others covering the 1988 Democratic National Convention.

Among the professoriate I picked the brains of Spencer Klaw, then editor of the *Columbia Journalism Review*; Richard M. Pious, Barnard; Herbert J. Gans, Luther P. Jackson, Jr., Robert Y. Shapiro, and Ethel Klein, Columbia; Michael Goldstein, Claremont-McKenna; John McGlennon, William and Mary; Merle Black and Philip Meyer, University of North Carolina; James David Barber, Duke; Earl Black and Don Fowler, University of South Carolina; Robert P. Steed, The Citadel; Stephen D. Shaffer and Douglas Feig, Mississippi State; Harold W. Stanley, University of Alabama; Charles D. Hadley, University of New Orleans; David L. Martin, Auburn; Ronald W. Walters, Howard; Gaither Loewenstein, Wright State; Lyttleton Sanders, Lamar University; and Marvin Kalb, Kennedy School, Harvard. I talked by phone with Larry Sabato, University of Virginia; Thomas F. Eamon, East Carolina University; and Thomas E. Cavanagh, National Research Council, National Academy of Sciences.

In addition to *Congressional Quarterly*, I followed the *Southern Political Report* and *The Polling Report*, using their contents constantly. I received copies of the CBS-*New York Times* exit polls thanks to Kathy Frankovic of CBS and Michael Kagay of the *Times*. ABC's polls were furnished by Stan Opotowsky and NBC's by Joseph Angotti. *Media Monitor* of the Center for Media and Public Affairs, Washington, collected useful data on TV news coverage of elections. Charley Williams, executive director, and Dan O'Conner, research associate, of the Southern Legislative Conference office in Atlanta kept me abreast of Super Tuesday official election and turnout figures.

In the course of my wanderings I visited the campaign headquarters of Michael Dukakis in Boston, Al Gore in Arlington, Virginia, Pat Robertson in Chesapeake, Virginia, and Paul Simon and George Bush in Washington. Julia Sutherland of the state Democratic Committee and Joe Elton of the state Republican Committee in Virginia helped me to understand the early days of the Super Tuesday campaign there. Scott Hatch and Mary Ellen Miller of the Robertson campaign instructed me in his telephone polling operation. On the campaign trail, I spent the evening of the South Carolina Republican primary in Bush headquarters in Columbia; the night before the Georgia primary in Jesse Jackson's Macon storefront; and the day of the South Carolina Democratic caucus in Jackson's home town, Greenville, with state senator Theo Walker Mitchell. Besides the Jackson state campaign coordinators quoted by name and in the "Debriefings" section at the end of this book, I talked with Ron Daniels, Jackson's Southern coordinator, and Randal Mangham in Jackson's Atlanta headquarters. Georgia state representative Calvin Smyre and North Carolina state representative Henry M. Michaux helped me to understand African-American politics in those states. Vee Stephenson of Jackson headquarters in Raleigh, North Carolina; Laura Scott, and city council member Lonnie Miley in Macon, Georgia; and Unnia Pettus of the National Rainbow Coalition's Washington office also lent a helping hand.

— P.K.

Index

Index

Index

About the Author

Penn Kimball has extensive experience in government and journalism. He served as staff aide to two state governors and a U.S. senator. He was formerly assistant to the Sunday editor of *The New York Times*, national affairs writer for *Time* magazine, and senior editor of *The New Republic*. His book *The File* was selected by the *Times* as one of the "most notable" of 1983 and became the basis of a BBC-Frontline documentary aired over the Public Broadcasting Service in 1987.

A graduate of Princeton, he received an M.A. in politics from Oxford, where he was a Rhodes Scholar, and a Ph.D. in political science from Columbia. He is the author of *The Disconnected*, a study of minority politics, *Bobby Kennedy and the New Politics,* and numerous articles in national magazines. He is professor emeritus at Columbia University's Graduate School of Journalism.

Other Titles of Interest
From the Joint Center Press . . .

Tom Bradley's Campaigns for Governor:
The Dilemma of Race and Political Strategies
by Thomas F. Pettigrew and Denise A. Alston (1988)

A Horse of a Different Color: Television's Treatment
of Jesse Jackson's 1984 Presidential Campaign
by C. Anthony Broh (1987)

Black Elected Officials—A National Roster: 1990